APPLIED RISK MANAGEMENT

the handbook for
# CAMPUS THREAT ASSESSMENT & MANAGEMENT TEAMS

by
**Gene Deisinger, Ph.D.**
**Marisa Randazzo, Ph.D.**
**Daniel O'Neill**
**Jenna Savage**

ISBN 10:        0-615-23493-3
ISBN 13: 978-0-615-23493-9


Cover art designed by Ellie Clayman

Set in Calibri

First Edition – November 2008

# TABLE OF CONTENTS

FOREWORD                                                                    v

AUTHORS OF THE HANDBOOK                                                    vii

ACKNOWLEDGEMENTS                                                           ix

INTRODUCTION                                                                1

SECTION 1: DEFINITION AND PURPOSE                                          7

SECTION 2: MISSION AND GUIDING PRINCIPLES                                 23

SECTION 3: TEAM COMPOSITION, ROLES AND RESPONSIBILITIES                   33

SECTION 4: THE THREAT ASSESSMENT AND MANAGEMENT PROCESS                   45

SECTION 5: TEAM OPERATIONS AND COMMUNICATION                              79

SECTION 6: INFORMATION SHARING AND RECORD KEEPING                         87

SECTION 7: ADDITIONAL INSTITUTION COMPONENTS                              95

CONCLUSION                                                                103

BIBLIOGRAPHY                                                              107

APPENDIX A: DECISION POINTS                                               113

APPENDIX B: CHECKLISTS                                                    119

APPENDIX C: QUICK REFERENCE GUIDES                                        133

APPENDIX D: SAMPLE POLICIES, PROCEDURES AND FORMS                         143

APPENDIX E: ADDITIONAL RESOURCES                                          159

# FOREWORD

Years ago, in the aftermath of a student suicide, I came across a message the victim had written to himself in the margins of one of his notebooks:

"Can I ever teach? Will I ever cure stuttering? Job interviews, phone calls. People notice *or am I blowing this out of proportion*?" [emphasis added].

In our subsequent interviews with the victim's friends, none of them thought he had a stuttering problem. He was indeed "blowing this out of proportion."

All of us have comparable internal debates, usually triggered by the powerful role of *fear* in framing the issues. Fear, of course, has an invaluable function. Our ancestors didn't have time for extensive cognition when leopards jumped out of the bush. But nature has also blessed or burdened us with a more recent evolutionary development: the prefrontal cortex. This part of the brain relies, in part, on reason to evaluate the nature and seriousness of a perceived threat. One price we pay for such complex neural architecture is doubt.

Experience has shown—at least when no immediate physical threat is present—that the capacity for thinking gives us the greatest margin of safety. The inevitable doubts that arise are best resolved by following the guidance of the prefrontal cortex ("higher self") rather than taking counsel of our fears.

This important handbook is mainly about *thinking*. And its premise is grounded in a thoughtful perspective. The authors state:

> The [threat assessment] *process is not, by default, adversarial in nature. The threat assessment and management process, where possible, attempts to help people, not punish them. Indeed, if the Team is informed early enough, it can get involved long before an individual may have done any wrongdoing, and prevent such incidents from ever occurring. (p. 25)*

Keeping that perspective in mind will help you design and implement a model threat assessment program. It will also allow you to see how the core components of threat assessment—fact-driven analysis, cross-functional cooperation, individualized assessment, and treating students the way we would want to be treated—also define our broader educational mission.

Gary Pavela
Editor, *The Pavela Report* and
*Law & Policy Report*

## AUTHORS OF THE HANDBOOK

**Gene Deisinger, Ph.D.**, is a nationally recognized expert on threat assessment and management. Dr. Deisinger was a founding member of the Iowa State University Critical Incident Response Team (CIRT), a multidisciplinary team that serves as a pro-active planning group and coordinates institutional responses during crisis situations. As part of this team, Dr. Deisinger developed the threat management program. He has served as the primary threat manager for Iowa State University since the program's inception in 1994. This program has been recognized as a model for threat assessment in college and university settings. He has personally managed and supervised threat cases and protective details for a broad range of governmental dignitaries, public figures, and members of the university community. Dr. Deisinger has provided consultation and training to numerous colleges, universities, law enforcement agencies, and private corporations across the United States, and has been an invited speaker for several national organizations. He currently serves as a subject matter expert, consulting to the FBI, Secret Service and U.S. Dept of Education, regarding their joint study of targeted violence in institutions of higher education. As a licensed psychologist, a certified health service provider in psychology, and a certified peace officer, Dr. Deisinger brings a unique perspective to the field of threat assessment. He serves as the Associate Director of Public Safety and Deputy Chief of Police with the Iowa State University Police Division, and also serves as a Special Deputy United States Marshal with the FBI Joint Terrorism Task Force.
*Email*: gdeisinger@ThreatResources.com

**Marisa Reddy Randazzo, Ph.D.**, is a national expert on threat assessment and targeted violence. Formerly the Chief Research Psychologist for the U.S. Secret Service, Dr. Randazzo has provided threat assessment training to over 10,000 professionals in higher education, secondary schools, corporations, law enforcement agencies, human resources, mental health, and the intelligence community throughout the United States, Canada, and the European Union. In her ten years with the Secret Service, she reviewed hundreds of threat investigations and supervised the agency's research on assassinations, presidential threats, insider threats, school shootings, security breaches, and stalking incidents. She also served as Co-Director of the Safe School Initiative, the largest

federal study of school shootings in the United States, and is co-author of the U.S. Secret Service/U.S. Department of Education model of threat assessment for educational institutions. Dr. Randazzo now heads Threat Assessment Resources International, LLC, providing threat assessment training and case consultation to colleges, schools, corporations, and security professionals. She has testified before Congress, briefed Cabinet Secretaries, and been interviewed by numerous major television, radio, and print news outlets about threat assessment and targeted violence prevention. In 2005, Dr. Randazzo was awarded the Williams College Bicentennial Medal for her work in preventing violence.
*Email*: MRR@ThreatResources.com   *Phone*: (775) 741-3314

**Daniel O'Neill** is the Founder, President and CEO of Applied Risk Management (ARM), LLC. ARM provides global risk management and security engineering services. Mr. O'Neill is a co-author of the report, *Campus Violence Prevention and Response: Best Practices for Massachusetts Higher Education*. He has been the Principal in Charge of over 100 security consulting engagements including multiple large scale university and college projects. He is a former U.S. Army Airborne Ranger and is a graduate of the Harvard Business School.
*Email*: doneill@arm-security.com   *Phone*: (877) 365-8880 x302

**Jenna Savage** is the Special Projects Manager for Applied Risk Management (ARM), LLC. She is a co-author of the report, *Campus Violence Prevention and Response: Best Practices for Massachusetts Higher Education*. Ms. Savage is a doctoral student in Criminology and Justice Policy at Northeastern University. Ms. Savage's dissertation research explores how gender differences in socialization can lead to subsequent differences in criminal and deviant behavior.
*Email*: jsavage@arm-security.com   *Phone*: (781) 640-6497

# ACKNOWLEDGEMENTS

The authors would like to thank the following people, without whom this Handbook would not have been possible: David B. Baty, for his leadership and assistance with logistics and scheduling; Jessica Lavin, for graphical design; Amy Talton, for marketing; Ellie Clayman, for the cover art; Peter Tsaffaras, for his support and guidance; Aaron Solar, for technical assistance; Jo Flanagan, for administrative and logistical support; and Gary Pavela, Catherine Cortez Masto, Gary Margolis, Michael Roberto, Steven Healy, and Jeff Nolan for their feedback and contributions to the development of this Handbook.

We are indebted to all those who have worked tirelessly to enhance the safety of campuses, schools and workplaces. We have benefited greatly from the knowledge, experience, and friendship of so many extraordinary professionals including: Randy Borum, Robert Fein, Loras Jaeger, Drew Leavens, Bob Martin, Reid Meloy, Bill Modzeleski, Kris Mohandie, Bill Pollack, Ray Thrower, Bryan Vossekuil, Stephen White, Roger Depue, James Alan Fox, Elizabeth Englander, and Linda Florence. They have challenged and inspired us in their commitment to understanding situations and preventing violence.

We also owe a debt of gratitude to our beloved family and friends, who have been very supportive and patient with us throughout this process. Gene would like to thank his wife Maureen, and his sons, Jason and Ryan for the gift of their love and support. Marisa would like to thank her husband, Robert, for his unending support, love, and humor. Dan would like to thank his wife, Cara, and his daughters, Lauren and Allie, for their love, laughter and support. And Jenna thanks Jamie Fox for his friendship and for providing so many opportunities over the years, and her family — Norm, Judy, Matt, and Lillian — for their love and support.

Finally, we thank the communities and organizations that we have been privileged to serve and protect.

# INTRODUCTION

# INTRODUCTION

The April 2007 massacre of 32 victims on the campus of Virginia Tech sent shockwaves through college and university communities across America. Not only was it one of the most devastating violent episodes ever to occur at an institution of higher learning, it was the largest mass shooting of any kind in our nation's history. In the wake of the shooting at Virginia Tech, and the shooting at Northern Illinois University ten months later, we heard the same questions over and over: How could this happen? What sort of person would do this? Where will it happen next, and when? How can we ever be safe? How can you ever stop a person that just snaps like that?

Understandable as these questions are, they are fueled by fear, misinformation, and misunderstanding about the process of violence in general, the dynamics of most campus attacks, and the dynamics of the perpetrators involved. This book aims to dispel such misinformation and fear and to replace them with factual information about what can be done to prevent the next campus attack. Based upon our research and years of practical case experience, we will outline the steps that campus personnel can take to identify and evaluate persons and situations that have raised some concern, intervene where necessary to prevent harm, and generally assist persons who may be struggling or in despair.

### Threat Assessment on Campus, Post-Virginia Tech

In the time since the shootings at Virginia Tech on April 16, 2007 and at Northern Illinois University on February 14, 2008, we have seen an overwhelming amount of media attention devoted to campus threats and campus security issues generally, leaving us with the sense that campus violence has reached epidemic proportions. We have seen numerous vendors offering an array of products purported to address campus security needs, including high-tech solutions to the question of which student will be the next campus shooter. We have seen some people, on campus and off, argue for allowing students, faculty, and staff to carry weapons on campus so that they may protect themselves and deter a would-be shooter. And we have seen much discussion — finally — about threat assessment on campus. An increasing number of higher educational institutions are looking at ways to use this process to identify and respond to students, faculty and staff who may pose a danger to others on campus, may pose a danger to themselves, or who simply may be struggling and in need of assistance and resources.

We say "finally" because we believe that threat assessment, or behavioral threat assessment as it is also known, provides an effective and low-cost solution to make campuses safer. It is a process that strives to treat everyone involved with fairness and respect, including persons who have raised concern through inappropriate behaviors and communications. Threat assessment was first proposed as a model for addressing risk of certain types of school violence shortly after the attack at Columbine High School.[1] Since the Virginia Tech shooting, the threat assessment model has been widely advocated for use in higher education settings by a broad array of entities at the federal and state levels, as well as various national associations.[2] Over 80 percent of all reports on college and university security published in the aftermath of the Virginia Tech shooting have recommended, in one form or another, that higher education institutions establish threat assessment teams.[3] And in 2008, the Commonwealth of Virginia and the State of Illinois both enacted laws requiring their colleges and universities to establish threat assessment teams.[4]

---

1   Fein, R., Vossekuil, B., Pollack, W., Borum, R., Modzeleski, W., & Reddy, M. (2002). *Threat assessment in schools: A guide to managing threatening situations and to creating safe school climates*. Washington, DC: U.S. Department of Education and U.S. Secret Service; Mohandie, K. (2000). *School violence threat management: A practical guide for educators, law enforcement, and mental health professionals*. San Diego, CA: Specialized Training Services; Reddy, M., Borum, R., Vossekuil, B., Fein, R., Berglund, J., & Modzeleski, W., (2001). Evaluating risk for targeted violence in schools: Comparing risk assessment, threat assessment, and other approaches. *Psychology in the Schools, 38*, pp. 157-172.

2   See e.g., International Association of Campus Law Enforcement Administrators (IACLEA) (2008). *Overview of the Virginia Tech tragedy and implications for campus safety: The IACLEA Blueprint for safer campuses*. West Hartford, CT: IACLEA; Leavitt, M., Spellings, M., & Gonzalez, A. (2007). *Report to the President on issues raised by the Virginia Tech tragedy*. Washington, DC: U.S. Department of Health and Human Services, U.S. Department of Education, and U.S. Department of Justice; National Association of Attorneys General (2007). *NAAG task force on school and campus safety: Report and recommendations*. Washington, DC: National Association of Attorneys General; Virginia Tech Review Panel (2007). *Mass shootings at Virginia Tech, April 16, 2007: Report of the Review Panel presented to Governor Kaine, Commonwealth of Virginia*. Richmond, VA: Authors.

3   For a complete listing of these reports and their recommendations, see O'Neill, D., Fox, J., Depue, R., Englander, E., et al. (2008). *Campus violence prevention and response: Best practices for Massachusetts Higher Education*. Boston, MA: Massachusetts Department of Higher Education. Available at *http://www.arm-security.com/pdf/ARM_MA_Colleges_ Campus_Violence_Prevention_And_Response.pdf*

4   Sluss, M. (2008, April 9). Governor signs Virginia Tech-inspired mental health reform bills. *The Roanoke Times, http://www.roanoke.com/news/breaking/wb/157560*, retrieved April 25, 2008; State Journal-Register (2008, August 22). *Gov. signs bill requiring emergency plans at colleges. http://www.sj-r.com/homepage/x633543415/Gov-signs-bill-requiring-emergency-plans-at-colleges*, retrieved October 22, 2008.

A Threat Assessment and Management Team (TAM Team) is a multidisciplinary team that is responsible for the careful and contextual identification and evaluation of behaviors that raise concern and that may precede violent activity on campus. The early identification of these "red flags" enables colleges and universities to prudently take the appropriate precautionary steps to prevent targeted violence from occurring. In addition, it also ensures that persons in need — whether they be students, faculty, staff, or other members of the community — are directed to the appropriate support mechanism on campus. By providing an environment that ensures both the physical safety and mental well-being of its community, colleges and universities can improve the overall quality of life on campus.

In our experience as threat assessment practitioners and researchers, we have seen threat assessment used effectively to prevent a wide array of harm on campus, not just the next "campus shooting." We have also seen it used to connect people-in-need with necessary resources to help resolve underlying problems that may lead them to consider or resort to violence in the first place. Threat assessment is a process that is decidedly low-cost and easy to implement, as many colleges and universities already possess the key resources — namely, a team of people who, with their connections throughout campus, can gather pieces of information and assemble them into a larger picture. At the heart of campus threat assessment is an effort to break down or work around silos where information might exist, and to provide a mechanism to collect and share that information. This facilitates a more comprehensive picture of what a person of concern is doing, saying, and considering, and enables the Team to develop and implement an integrated management strategy to address those concerns. Finally, the Team is then able to follow up with that strategy through the resolution of those concerns.

### Handbook Overview

The purpose of this Handbook is to assist colleges and universities with the establishment, conduct, and effective operation of a TAM Team. Our goal is to provide guidance for the development and implementation of an effective TAM Team, and to explain the guiding principles and key practices of campus threat assessment and management. We also provide a detailed discussion about how the threat assessment and management process works.

In Section One, we briefly discuss what a TAM Team is and why such a team is necessary. In Section Two, we discuss the mission and guiding principles of threat assessment and management. In Section Three, we present our recommendations regarding the composition of a TAM Team, and also discuss team members' specific roles and responsibilities. In Section Four, we explain the process of threat assessment and management. In Section Five, we provide guidance regarding how and when to conduct threat assessment meetings, including managing cases, training, and strategic planning. In Section Six, we discuss the importance of keeping records and also examine issues of privacy and confidentiality. Finally, in Section Seven, we provide information about additional campus components that can complement a TAM Team's work. Following the Conclusion, we include several appendices that contain checklists, quick reference guides, sample policies and procedures, and other related resources.

It is important to note that every TAM Team is different. While this Handbook is intended to provide guidance, there are very few hard-set rules that all teams must follow in the day-to-day practice of their efforts. Rather, each team should consider the unique needs of its campus community — which may vary greatly depending upon the institution's size, location, population, and various other factors — as well as resources that the institution may already have in place that could be harnessed to assist the threat assessment and management process. For this reason, we highlight what we refer to as "Decision Points" throughout this Handbook. These are questions for which there is no single answer, but ones that each TAM Team must consider in light of the needs of that team's particular institution.

Finally, the information in this book is intended to serve as principles and parameters for those interested in threat assessment in higher education settings. It is not intended as a rigid set of procedures, nor as an exhaustive set of solutions. Each case and situation that a threat assessment team encounters is different and requires an individualized and case-specific approach. What works for one institution or one case may not work for another. We encourage all who read this book to consult their colleagues at other institutions and subject matter experts whenever necessary.

# SECTION ONE

## DEFINITION AND PURPOSE

## DEFINITION AND PURPOSE

### Context of Campus Violence and Crime

Since April 2007, we have experienced a nearly overwhelming amount of media attention devoted to campus threats and campus security issues, generally leaving us with the sense that campus violence has reached epidemic proportions. The reality, however, is that the likelihood of a shooting or homicide on campus remains extremely low. As can be seen in Table 1, other, more common crimes continue to account for most incidents of violence on college and university campuses.

**Table 1: On-Campus Violence, 2004 – 2006**

| Type of Violence | 2004 | 2005 | 2006 |
|---|---|---|---|
| Murder | 16 | 11 | 8 |
| Forcible sex | 2,675 | 2,704 | 2,704 |
| Robbery | 1,982 | 2,028 | 1,969 |
| Aggravated assault | 2,914 | 2,868 | 3,070 |
| Arson | 1,068 | 1,019 | 970 |
| Injurious hate crimes | 17 | 21 | 12 |
| Illegal weapon possession | 1,314 | 1,425 | 1,415 |

*Source: U.S. Department of Education (September, 2008)[5]*

Homicidal violence of any type — and mass attacks in particular — are rare on college campuses. While we should strive to prevent such extreme violence through every reasonable means, we must understand that there is a broader context of violence in society and on campuses as well. Table 1 illustrates some of this range of violence from the unlawful possession of a weapon to acts of physical and sexual assault and, ultimately, homicide. Homicide is but the tip of the iceberg of violent behavior. We must not lose sight of the rest of the "iceberg" simply because the tip is so much more apparent and frightening. The safety of a campus community is impacted on a much more regular, and perhaps more insidious, basis through the occurrence of those lesser acts of

5   Summary national crime statistics for colleges and universities for 2004-2006, posted on the U.S. Department of Education website. Retrieved October 30, 2008 at *http://www.ed.gov/admins/lead/safety/criminal-04-06.pdf.*

violence. Any approach that seeks only to deal with homicidal violence will be found lacking as the community seeks to find and maintain a sense of safety and security.

Note also that the data in Table 1 do not address other behaviors that can be highly disruptive to the safe and effective operation of a campus community. Behaviors such as threatening statements, intimidating comments or behaviors, or patterns of bullying have a pervasive and on-going impact upon campus safety, but are not well researched or documented. This range of behaviors from bullying to homicidal acts represents the true range of violence on campus or any workplace. This is the context and the domain in which threat assessment practices may be more fully applied.

### Threat Assessment and Mental Health Issues

In addition to violence on campus, another serious concern for colleges and universities is the apparently increasing proportion of students with mental health conditions who may require some assistance or monitoring to complete their degree safely and successfully. As shown in Table 2, campus counseling centers are dealing with several serious issues that could have an impact on the safety and well-being of the entire campus.

**Table 2: Mental Health on Campus**

| Counseling Center Dealing With: | Percent |
|---|---|
| Obsessive Pursuit Cases* | 38 |
| Hospitalization of Student | 87 |
| Student Suicide | 26 |
| Client Suicide | 22 |
| Percent of clients referred for psychiatric evaluation | 15 |
| Percent of clients prescribed psychiatric medications | 23 |

Source: 2007 National Survey of Counseling Center Directors[6]
* 271 cases of obsessive pursuit were reported, with 80 students being injured and 9 being killed by their pursuer

6    Gallagher, R. (2007). National Survey of Counseling Center Directors 2007. Alexandria, VA: International Association of Counseling Services, Inc.

As this table shows, over a third of college and university counseling centers reported involvement in situations in which students were victims of unwanted or obsessive pursuit. While not all of these cases would likely meet criminal definitions of stalking, it is clear that many of these situations represented significant danger to the persons involved, as indicated by the number of victims being injured or killed by those engaged in the pursuit behaviors. Such situations tend to be complex, rapidly changing and best handled through a multidisciplinary approach.

Many centers reported involvement in the hospitalization of students, most frequently because the student's behaviors represented a risk of imminent harm to themselves (rather than others), or a greatly diminished ability to care for their basic survival needs. Suicide is the second leading cause of death among college students, with an estimated 1,100 students killing themselves every year.[7]

Not only must colleges and universities ensure that their campuses are physically safe and procedurally sound, but they must also take steps to provide for the mental well-being of their community. The vast majority of mentally ill persons will never become violent, much less perpetrate a mass shooting. Nevertheless, mental illness can include behaviors that may be harmful to the individual and/or disruptive to the entire campus community, such as suicidal ideation and attempts, self-injurious behavior, inappropriate aggression, and alcohol or other drug abuse. Therefore, colleges and universities must take every step they can to respond to the mental health needs of their community. Developing a TAM Team can help an institution address all of these issues.

As Table 3 shows, mental health professionals have noted an increase in various troubling behaviors in recent years.

---

7    Suicide Prevention Resource Center (2004). *Promoting mental health and preventing suicide in college and university settings.* Newton, MA: Education Development Center, Inc.

## Table 3: Mental Health on Campus

| Counseling Center Directors Reporting Increases in: | Percent |
|---|---|
| Students with severe psychological problems | 91 |
| Students coming to college with psychiatric medication(s) | 88 |
| Students seeking counseling | 11 |
| Students being victims of relationship violence | 41 |
| Students engaging in self-injurious behaviors | 58 |
| Students being victims of sexual assault | 16 |
| Students experiencing problems due to alcohol abuse | 48 |
| Calls from parents regarding services for students | 23 |
| Other drug problems | 39 |

*Source: 2007 National Survey of Counseling Center Directors[8]*

In 2007, the National Survey of Counseling Center Directors found that nearly half (49%) of all counseling center clients had severe mental health issues, including depression, anxiety, panic attacks, and suicidal ideation.[9] It is important to note, however, that the majority of those students with severe mental health issues were able to safely and effectively continue their enrollment as students. Fewer than 20% of students with major mental health concerns were so impaired that they could not maintain their enrollment. Clearly, a "one size fits all" approach to identifying and responding to persons with mental health concerns is not appropriate or helpful. Effective responses are based on individualized assessment of the student and their situation in order to help determine what is best for that student AND for the community as a whole.

### *Definition of a Threat Assessment and Management Team*
The TAM Team is a multidisciplinary team that interacts and operates on a regular basis — and as needed for crisis situations. The Team is available to review and discuss any students, employees or other persons who have raised concern and may be at risk of harming either themselves or others, or who pose a significant disruption to the learning, living or working environment. This team receives and assesses all reports of threats and other alarming behaviors by any student or employee of a college or university, as well as by others who might impact the safety or

---

8    Gallagher, 2007.
9    Gallagher, 2007.

well-being of the campus community (e.g., people living within close proximity of the campus who are exhibiting threatening or unusual behaviors). It is the Team's responsibility to evaluate the legitimacy of concerns reported to it, assess the likelihood that an individual may cause harm to himself/herself or others (or pose a significant disruption), develop strategies for reducing the risk, implement these strategies, and then monitor and re-evaluate the situation to ensure that they have been effective.

As we mentioned in the Introduction, nearly every national, state, and professional association review on campus and school security conducted since the Virginia Tech shooting has recommended or supported the use of threat assessment to prevent violence.[10] It is important to note, however, that while these reviews and recommendations for threat assessment teams are new, several campuses have employed threat assessment models for many years.[11] Campus threat assessment is not a new methodology; rather, it is an adaptation of methodologies that have been around for many years with foundations in workplace violence prevention programs, Secret Service protective intelligence models, and student development approaches to dealing with students in crisis.[12]

---

### _Decision Point_: **What should you call your team?**

Each college and university must decide what it would like to call its threat assessment and management team. Many institutions may simply prefer to call their team a "Threat Assessment Team." Others may be concerned that incorporating the term "threat" may make the team seem less approachable, less supportive, or may connote an adversarial process, which goes against one of the guiding principles of threat assessment and management. Therefore, another name may be chosen. For example, we prefer the title "Threat Assessment and Management Team" because it draws attention to the

---

10  E.g., IACLEA, 2008; NAAG, 2007; O'Neill et al., 2008

11  Dunkle, J., Silverstein, Z. & Warner, S. (2008).  Managing violent and other troubling students: The role of threat assessment on campus. _Journal of College and University Law, 34(3),_ 585-636.

12  See e.g., Dunkle, Silverstein & Warner, 2008; Fein, R. & Vossekuil, B. (1998). _Protective intelligence and threat assessment investigations: A guide for state and local law enforcement officials._ Washington, DC: U.S. Department of Justice, Office of Justice Programs, National Institute of Justice; Turner, J. & Gelles, M. (2003), _Threat assessment: A risk management approach._ Binghamton, NY: Haworth Press; Delworth, U. (1989).  Dealing with the behavioral and psychological problems of students. _New Directions for Student Services,_ no. 45. San Francisco: Jossey-Bass.

management function of the team, which is extremely important and may be overlooked by focusing solely on assessment. Other names that have been used include:

- Student Assistance Team
- Early Alert Team
- Behavioral Intervention Team
- Students of Concern
- Student Intervention Team
- Staff Intervention Team
- Campus Assistance Team
- Care Team

The team's name should reflect the values of the institution and the mission of the team. For instance, if the team will only be focusing on threats posed by students, then a name with "Student" in the title is appropriate. Whatever its name, the team should go beyond the function of a traditional student assistance team and incorporate the threat assessment methodology discussed in this Handbook.

### The Purpose of Threat Assessment and Management

The main goals of the TAM Team are to prevent individuals from harming either themselves or others, and generally to assist persons in need. These persons include not only students, but also a college or university's faculty, staff, and all other members of the campus community, as well as persons not affiliated with the campus who may pose a threat. Unlike many other steps that institutions of higher education may take to improve the security of their campus community, such as implementation of a mass notification system, installing outdoor warning systems, and training law enforcement officers in rapid deployment to active shooter scenarios, threat management focuses on *preventing* violence, rather than solely responding to it.

By identifying and responding to persons in need, the TAM Team is perhaps the most critical tool that a college or university can use to prevent targeted violence on campus, as well as identify and intervene with other problems that affect the health and well-being of the campus community such as suicide and drug/alcohol abuse. By the term "targeted violence," we are referring to violence that is premeditated and aimed at specific target(s) selected prior to the incident.[13] More specifically, targeted violence can be defined as "violent incidents where both the perpetrator and target(s) are identified or identifiable prior to the incident."[14] For example, violence that might spontaneously erupt in the midst of a volatile intimate relationship is unlikely to be preventable through the work of a TAM Team. However, an ex-boyfriend who becomes depressed and suicidal after a break-up and begins stalking his ex-girlfriend may be prevented from harming her or himself through a TAM Team's intervention.

Long before many perpetrators of targeted violence act out, they often raise "red flags" among various individuals with whom they come in contact, including professors, police, peers, and mental health counselors.[15] The problem is that this information is often scattered among multiple individuals. Moreover, these various individuals often do not communicate with each other about their concerns. Therefore, no one person has a full picture of what is going on with the person who has raised some concern. As Peter Lake, Director of the Center for Excellence in Higher Education Law and Policy, and Professor of Law at Stetson University, noted:

> *Most important, dangerous people rarely show all of their symptoms to just one department or group on campus. A professor may see a problem in an essay, the campus police may endure belligerent statements, a resident assistant may notice the student is a loner, the counseling center may notice that the student fails to appear for a follow-up visit. Acting independently, no department is likely to solve the problem. In short, colleges must recognize that managing an educational environment is a team effort, calling for collaboration and multilateral solutions.[16]*

---

13  Borum, Fein, Vossekuil, & Berglund (1999). Threat assessment: Defining an approach for evaluating risk of targeted violence. *Behavioral Sciences & the Law, 17*, 323-337. See also Fein & Vossekuil (1998); Fein, R., Vossekuil, B. & Holden, G. (September, 1995).  Threat assessment: An approach to prevent targeted violence. *Research in Action, 1-7.*  Washington, DC: U.S. Department of Justice, Office of Justice Programs, National Institute of Justice.

14  Reddy et al., 2001; pages 157-158.

15  Vossekuil, B., Fein, R., Reddy, M., Borum, R., & Modzeleski, W. (2002). *The final report and findings of the Safe School Initiative: Implications for the prevention of school attacks in the United States.* Washington, DC: U.S. Department of Education and U.S. Secret Service.

16  Lake, P. F. (June 2007). Higher education called to account: Colleges and the law after Virginia Tech. *Chronicle of Higher Education, 53*(43), B6.

Without such a team effort, the extent of the threat posed by the person in question may remain unknown until it is too late to intervene and to prevent escalation where possible.

### Virginia Tech Case Study

In its review of the Virginia Tech shooting, the Virginia Governor's Review Panel uncovered numerous pieces of information about Seung-Hui Cho and his behavior prior to his attack.[17] The Review Panel concluded that much was known about Cho's troubling behavior prior to his attack, but that the information was scattered throughout different departments and personnel on campus. There was no one person or entity at the Virginia Tech campus who was looking for or knew all of the available pieces of information.

Before proceeding to discuss what scattered information was known about Cho prior to the attack, we must emphasize that the problems seen in the Virginia Tech case are typical of the problems and weaknesses regarding information sharing and follow-up at institutions across the country. While the Review Panel report provides some of the clearest documentation of these types of problematic patterns, the circumstances described within their report are in no way unique to Virginia Tech.

The Review Panel indicated that the following people and entities had raised concerns about Cho prior to his attack:[18]

1.  *Cho's roommate and suitemates*: They invited him out on a few occasions, but stopped doing so after they went to a girl's room and Cho took out a knife and started stabbing the carpet. His suitemates also stopped inviting him to meals because he never spoke. Cho would call his suite from phones around campus, tell whoever answered that he was "question mark" — Cho's twin brother — and ask to speak to Cho.

2.  *Creative Writing professor*: She observed Cho to be uncooperative and disruptive in class. He would wear reflective sunglasses to class and a hat that he pulled down over his eyes, and he refused to take them off until the professor stood by his desk. His professor learned that Cho had also been taking pictures of his female classmates under their desks, using his cell phone.

3.  *Creative Writing classmates*: Cho read aloud one of his creative writing pieces in class and it disturbed his classmates because of its

---

17  Virginia Tech Review Panel, 2007.
18  Virginia Tech Review Panel, 2007.

violent content. Some stopped coming to class because they were scared of Cho.

4.  *Chair of the English Department*: Cho's Creative Writing professor spoke with the chair of the English Department about Cho's writings, his behavior in class, and its impact on her other students.

5.  *Various administrators*: The English Department chair raised the above concerns with several people, including the Dean of Student Affairs, the College of Liberal Arts, the university's counseling center, and the director of Judicial Affairs. The counseling center said that Cho's writings contained no specific threat, but they recommended that Cho be referred to the counseling center. The director of Judicial Affairs also told the English Department chair that the content of Cho's writing was "inappropriate and alarming, but doesn't contain a threat to anyone's immediate safety (thus not actionable under the abusive conduct – threats section of the UPSL" (university code of student conduct).[19]

6.  *Campus "Care Team"*: Cho was discussed by Virginia Tech's "Care Team," a team of university personnel that addressed students who appeared to be in need of counseling or mental health care, at one of their regular meetings. The Care Team was informed that the English Department chair suggested that she tutor Cho privately as a way to handle Cho's behavior. The Care Team perceived that the situation was taken care of and did nothing further. They did not refer Cho to the counseling center. They never discussed Cho again, nor was the Care Team alerted later in the semester when both the Virginia Tech police department and Residence Life became aware of Cho stalking and scaring two female students.

7.  *Student pursued by Cho*: A female student complained to the university police department that Cho was scaring her, sending her text messages, showing up at her room in sunglasses and a hat pulled down over his eyes, and telling her his name was "question mark."

8.  *Campus police, first contact*: The Virginia Tech police told Cho not to bother the female student anymore and reported him to Judicial Affairs.

9.  *Resident Advisor*: Cho's resident advisor learned that Cho's roommate and suitemates found a very large knife in Cho's desk and threw it away.

---

19  Virginia Tech Review Panel, 2007; p. 43.

10. *Counseling Center, first contact*: Cho called the counseling center and made an appointment to see the counselor that the English Department chair has recommended. Cho did not keep the appointment.

11. *Judicial Affairs*: The assistant director of Judicial Affairs was notified about Cho's "odd behavior" and "stalking."[20] No report was made to the Care Team.

12. *Second female student pursued by Cho*: A second female student had received several instant messages and postings on her *Facebook.com* webpage during the semester that she believed were from Cho. The tone of the notes was self-deprecating and she would respond with efforts to make him feel better about himself. She asked several times if the writer was Cho but the response she got back was "I don't know who I am."[21] She also found a quote from *Romeo and Juliet* on the white board on the door to her room, which she also believed was from Cho. She asked her father what to do and he advised that she talk with the university police, which she did.

13. *Campus police, second contact*: Virginia Tech police met with Cho and told him not to have any more contact with the second female student. The Review Panel determined that many people were aware of this incident, including resident advisors, residential life staff, the director of Residence Life, and the assistant director of Judicial Affairs.

14. *Suitemate*: Following his conversation with university police, Cho sent an instant message to one of his suitemates that he "might as well kill himself."[22] Cho's suitemate reported this to the university police.

15. *Campus police, third contact*: University police returned to Cho's suite to talk with him again. They took Cho to the university police department for a pre-screen evaluation.[23] A licensed clinical social worker evaluated Cho, assessed him as mentally ill and a danger to himself or others, and recommended involuntary hospitalization. She contacted the magistrate, who issued a temporary detention order for Cho. Cho was hospitalized at a local psychiatric facility overnight.

---

20  Virginia Tech Review Panel, 2007; p. 44.

21  Virginia Tech Review Panel, 2007; p. 46.

22  Virginia Tech Review Panel, 2007; p. 47.

23  This example helps to demonstrate the critical role that law enforcement plays in threat assessment and other prevention efforts. Through strategies such as health and welfare visits, as well as other interactions, law enforcement may become aware early on of persons who are beginning to raise concern and can refer those persons to the campus TAM Team for further inquiry or to a mental health facility for emergency evaluation, even in cases where there is no criminal violation.

16. *Special Magistrate*: Cho was ordered by the court to undergo outpatient psychiatric treatment, which he was allowed to pursue through the university counseling center.[24] A facility representative helped Cho make an appointment with the counseling center for that same day.

17. *Counseling Center, second contact*: Cho kept his appointment at the counseling center but made no follow-up appointment. Because he was a voluntary patient at the university counseling center, he was not required to make a follow-up appointment. Neither the court nor the psychiatric facility was notified that Cho never returned to the university counseling center for further treatment.

18. *Other professors*: Cho took another Creative Writing course with a different professor and again concerned the professor because of the violent content of his writing assignments and his refusal to participate in class. Cho wrote one assignment for class that described a student who felt alienated from the rest of the campus and was going to carry out a killing spree in a classroom building but ultimately could not do so. Cho also took a playwriting class where his professor noted some of his assignments appeared to vent anger. Fellow students in this class discussed among themselves that they were waiting for Cho to "do something," with one student describing Cho as "the kind of guy who might go on a rampage killing."[25]

In addition to the information about Cho that was known to multiple personnel and students throughout the Virginia Tech campus, there was a wealth of information about his behavior in the years before he attended college that was known to Cho's parents, his former therapists, and to the personnel at his high school and middle school. This behavior included Cho writing a disturbing essay about how he wanted to carry out a Columbine-style attack at his school, after which he was diagnosed with clinical depression and treated successfully with psychiatric medication and ongoing monitoring by his parents, teachers, and therapists. But this information was not sought by anyone at Virginia Tech, nor by the

---

24  A systemic issue in the case of Cho at Virginia Tech was that the Virginia Tech counseling center did not accept court-ordered referrals in the first place (a common philosophy in college counseling centers), and was not informed of the order by the court. The counseling center staff members were unaware that Cho had been referred to them for treatment. According to the 2006 National Survey of Counseling Center Directors, only 39.8% of directors accept mandatory referrals for both assessment and counseling; 47.4% of directors accept mandated referrals for assessment purposes only and 12% accept no mandated referrals.

25  Virginia Tech Review Panel, 2007; p. 51

mental health agency that evaluated him when he was brought in by university police.

Virginia Tech had a well-developed Care Team that was intended to assist students having difficulties. But this team looked only at the particulars of a given incident or a particular point in time, and did not seek out nor obtain a comprehensive understanding of Cho's overall condition. The Review Panel noted that the Care Team was hampered by several factors, including the "absence of someone on the team who was experienced in threat assessment and knew to investigate the situation more broadly, checking for collateral information that would help determine if [Cho] truly posed a risk or not."[26] The Review Panel concluded that the Care Team "was ineffective in connecting the dots or heeding the red flags that were so apparent with Cho."[27]

This case helps to illustrate why a TAM Team is so vitally important. The TAM Team serves as a centralized location where an individual can report alarming behavior or troubled suspicions. Based upon an initial report, the Team can gather more information from others who know the person in question, piecing together scattered fragments to create a more comprehensive picture of the individual and the threat that he/she may pose. Armed with this information, the TAM Team can then develop a strategy to monitor the situation or intervene with the person if necessary to reduce the threat. The TAM Team facilitates communication, collaboration and coordination that can markedly improve the institution's response to developing concerns.

---

### A Word about Threat Assessment and Profiling

In the wake of the school shooting at Columbine High School, there was considerable discussion about using profiling to predict which students may become school shooters.[28] This discussion resumed after the Virginia Tech shooting with concern over identifying the next "campus shooter." We believe it is important to clarify here what is meant by profiling and how threat assessment and profiling differ.

When talking about predicting whether someone might become a "school shooter" or "workplace shooter," the term "profiling" refers

---

26  Virginia Tech Review Panel, 2007; p. 52.
27  Virginia Tech Review Panel, 2007; p. 52.
28  Reddy et al., 2001.

to comparing the person who has raised some concern with other perpetrators who have carried out the same types of attacks in the past — in terms of their demographic characteristics, background histories, what they look like (e.g. a "Goth" student), etc.[29] Based on an individual's *traits* in comparison to those characteristics that have been associated with violent individuals in the past, profiling attempts to determine the likelihood that a person will become violent in the future. While threat assessment is focused on *preventing* violence, profiling is focused on *predicting* violence. In this way, profiling is theoretical in nature.

Because profiling focuses on characteristics rather than behaviors, there is a tendency to make assumptions that individuals who possess certain traits will become violent.[30] This bias tends to produce a high rate of false positives and unwarranted stigmatization, since many individuals possess these traits but very few of them actually engage in targeted acts of violence.[31] Moreover, by focusing on a profile, it is possible to miss someone whose behavior suggests they are thinking about or planning for harm but who does not match or "fit" the profile.[32] By contrast, threat assessment is fact-based, focusing just on the information in the individual case and whether the facts gathered indicate the person is thinking about or planning harm. In this way, threat assessment is a deductive process — focusing on what conclusions the facts allow the Team to draw.[33] A TAM Team uses the information gathered both to assess whether the person in question poses a threat, and more importantly, to determine how best to intervene to prevent violence. Focused solely on prediction, profiling offers no guidance with respect to intervention or threat reduction.

---

29  Reddy et al., 2001.
30  Randazzo, M., Borum, R., Vossekuil, B., Fein, R., Modzeleski, W., & Pollack, W. (2006). Threat assessment in schools: Empirical support and comparison with other approaches. In S.R. Jimerson and M.J. Furlong (Eds.), The handbook of school violence and school safety: From research to practice. Mahwah, NJ: Lawrence Erlbaum Associates, Inc.; Reddy et al., 2001.
31  Randazzo et al., 2006; Reddy et al., 2001.
32  Randazzo et al., 2006; Reddy et al., 2001.
33  Randazzo et al., 2006; Reddy et al., 2001.

# SECTION TWO

## MISSION AND GUIDING PRINCIPLES

## MISSION AND GUIDING PRINCIPLES

The TAM Team's mission is to assess whether individuals pose a threat to themselves or others and intervene where necessary, and more generally to identify and provide assistance to those in need. The process is not, by default, adversarial in nature. The threat assessment and management process, where possible, attempts to help people, not punish them. Indeed, if the Team is informed early enough, it can get involved long before an individual may have done any wrongdoing, and prevent such incidents from ever occurring. Oftentimes, the TAM Team works together with the individual of concern, who can provide valuable feedback and proactively assist in the threat management process. The Team recognizes that individuals who most often come to its attention are those who are going through a difficult time in their lives and may be in need of help. While focused on protecting the community at large, the steps taken by the TAM Team are usually in the best interest of the individual in question as well. The Team aims not only to prevent people from harming others, but also from harming themselves or disrupting their own ability to succeed in their employment or educational goals. Many perpetrators of serious violence are, at some earlier point, often desperate or suicidal.[34] If these issues can be addressed and managed early enough, others will not be endangered.

As mentioned earlier, the TAM Team should focus not only on concerns about students, but also on concerns regarding a college or university's faculty and staff. It is important to keep in mind that colleges and universities are workplaces as well as learning institutions. Faculty and staff members often engage in behaviors that warrant the Team's attention. Even where students are the subjects of concerning behaviors, faculty and staff are still impacted (and vice versa). Therefore, we recommend a TAM Team with a comprehensive approach to assessing and managing any threats that impact upon the campus community.

In order to clarify its goals and purpose, and to make these known to the entire campus community, each TAM Team should have a written Mission Statement that is available to the public.

---

34  Vossekuil et al., 2002.

*Sample Mission Statement*

*The Threat Assessment and Management Team is committed to improving community safety through a proactive, collaborative, coordinated, objective, and thoughtful approach to the prevention, identification, assessment, intervention, and management of situations that pose, or may reasonably pose, a threat to the safety and well-being of the campus community.*

The Team should also have a strategic plan that sets forth how it intends to accomplish its mission. The strategic plan does not need to be complicated or overly detailed, but it should be congruent with the institution's campus-wide safety plan. The purpose of the strategic plan is to serve as a guide for the Team's overall operations, and to serve as a reminder of the Team's purpose when it gets caught up in day-to-day minutiae (see Section Five for further discussion of strategic plans).

### *Guiding Principles of Threat Assessment and Management*
There are twelve principles that guide threat assessment and management.[35]

### Principle 1:  Targeted Violence Can Often Be Prevented
The first guiding principle of threat assessment and management is that many incidents of targeted violence are preventable.[36] This principle is based upon data from school and workplace shootings that show that such targeted violence is rarely spontaneous. Rather, the perpetrator usually engages in a frequently observable pattern of thought and behavior prior to becoming violent. The perpetrator, often in response to a real or perceived grievance, will:

1.  come up with an idea to do harm (Ideation),

2.  develop a plan to carry out that harm (Planning),

3.  develop the capacity to carry out the plan, including getting access to weapons and ammunition (Preparation), and

4.  carry out the attack (Implementation).[37]

---

35  These principles come from Fein et al. (2002); Calhoun, F. & Weston, S. (June 2006). Protecting judicial officials: Implementing an effective threat management process. *Bureau of Justice Assistance Bulletin, 1-8.*  Washington, DC: U.S. Department of Justice, Office of Justice Programs, Bureau of Justice Assistance; and from the experience of the primary authors.

36  E.g., Fein & Vossekuil, 1998; Fein et al., 2002.

37  Vossekuil et al., 2002.

This process is illustrated in Figure 1. A TAM Team looks for information that may indicate that a person is on such a trajectory or pathway toward violence, and if such information is found, the Team then determines where it might be able to intervene to prevent harm.[38]

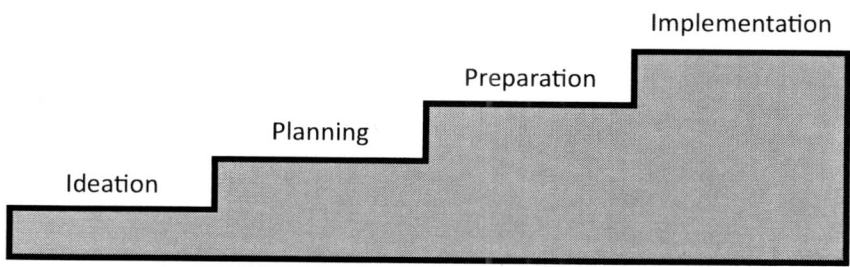

**Figure 1: The Escalation of Attack-Related Behaviors**[39]

By proactively identifying the behaviors that precede the escalation of targeted violence, the TAM Team can attempt to stop the forward progression down that pathway.[40]

### Principle 2: Violence is a Dynamic Process

The process of threat assessment and management is based on the understanding that violence is a dynamic process, rather than a static event or a state of being. A TAM Team does not try to determine whether someone is a "violent person" or not; rather, the Team tries to determine the circumstances or situation in which the person in question might pose a threat to themselves or others.[41] A key aspect of the threat assessment and management process is to look ahead over the coming days, weeks, and months and see what factors in a person's life might change — and if such changes might increase or decrease the likelihood of violence.[42] The particular threat posed by an individual of concern varies with the ebb and flow of his/her situation and the interventions that may be applied. The Team must continually monitor and re-evaluate the situation to maintain a clear awareness of the threat posed and the actual impact of the interventions used.

---

38  Fein et al., 2002.
39  Compiled from the following sources: Fein, et al., 2002; Calhoun, F. & Weston, S. (2003) *Contemporary threat management: A practical guide for identifying, assessing, and managing individuals of violent intent.* San Diego, CA. Specialized Training Services; and Calhoun & Weston, June 2006.
40  Fein et al., 2002.
41  Randazzo et al., 2006.
42  E.g., Fein et al., 2002.

## Principle 3:  Targeted Violence is a Function of Several Factors

Incidents of targeted violence arise from an intersection of several factors, including the individual of concern, their situation, the setting (i.e., influences on the individual's behavior), and the target of the individual's animosity or grievances.[43] Figure 2 illustrates this interaction. Threat assessment should not focus solely on the individual, but should also take into consideration all of these factors. The TAM Team must examine the context and the environment in which the individual lives, the individual's current situation, the factors that may precipitate violence or other negative behavior, and ways to make a target less accessible or vulnerable. It is possible that an individual's behavior is merely a symptom of some broader, systemic problem that needs to be addressed. Indeed, in many cases, the individual in question may have legitimate concerns, yet has behaved inappropriately in response to a particular stressor (e.g., threatened someone out of extreme frustration triggered by a situation that most reasonable persons would find stressful). The inappropriate behavior (the threat) must still be addressed. However, in order to prevent the subject of concern from doing any future harm, the best solution may be to facilitate a means of addressing and resolving the precipitating stressful situation.

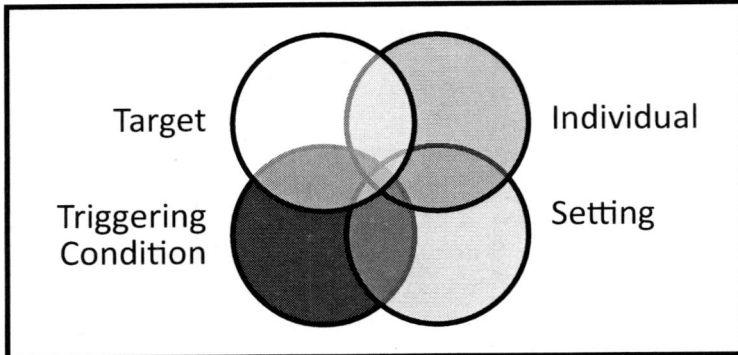

**Figure 2: Components of Risk**

## Principle 4:  Corroboration is Critical

Being skeptical about information received and corroborating information through multiple sources are critical to successful threat assessment and management.[44] This means that it is important to check facts where possible. It is quite likely that the TAM Team may hear one thing from the

---

43   Fein et al., 2002; Randazzo et al., 2006.
44   Fein et al., 2002.

individual in question, and something else entirely from another source, such as a roommate or colleague. Keeping a skeptical mindset enables the Team to gather and piece together various bits of information, weigh the credibility of each source, use the information to determine whether the individual poses a legitimate threat, and if so, to then find the best way to manage this threat. The threat assessment and management process is based upon facts and behaviors, not assumptions. The Team must be diligent in identifying and verifying original source information in order to maintain an objective view of the totality of the situation.

## Principle 5:  Threat Assessment is about Behavior, not Profiles

A major guiding principle of threat assessment is the notion that there is no single "type" of person who perpetrates targeted violence.[45] Instead, threat assessment is evidence-based, focusing on the specific behaviors a person has exhibited and determining whether the person poses a threat (or is at risk) based upon those behaviors.[46] Only by carefully assessing each individual (and situation) and the available evidence in each specific case does the TAM Team determine the appropriate response. It is this focus on behavior and the facts of a particular case that separates threat assessment from profiling. The focus in threat assessment is on what _this_ individual in _this_ particular context has done (or is doing) that causes concern.[47] (See box in Section One for discussion of threat assessment vs. profiling.)

## Principle 6:  Cooperating Systems are Critical Resources

Communication, collaboration, and coordination among various departments and agencies are critical throughout the process of threat assessment and management.[48] Having the participation of people from various parts of the campus, as well as the outside community, can enhance the major components of the threat assessment process: identifying persons of concern, gathering and sharing information, determining whether the person poses a threat (or is at risk), and, if necessary, developing and implementing an individualized case management plan to reduce the threat posed. Using different systems throughout campus as well as outside resources provides more eyes and ears on the process of both assessing and managing a potentially violent situation. Effective communication is necessary for the receipt, assessment, and response to critical information. Collaboration involves

---

45  Vossekuil et al., 2002.
46  Randazzo et al., 2006; Reddy et al., 2001.
47  Randazzo et al., 2006; Reddy et al., 2001.
48  E.g., Fein et al., 2002.

establishing effective relationships and a shared mission to achieve desired safety goals. Coordination involves prioritization and timing of interventions by differing members of the Team in order to implement and maximize the effectiveness of the management plan.

## Principle 7:  Does the Person Pose a Threat?

The central question of a threat assessment is whether the person in question _poses_ a threat, NOT solely whether he/she _made_ a threat.[49] A person makes a threat when he/she expresses intent to harm a target, whereas a person poses a threat when he/she "engag[es] in behavior that indicates furthering a plan or building capacity for a violent act."[50] This guiding principle of threat assessment means that a TAM Team should take all potential threatening behaviors seriously, not just those that have been verbalized or expressed in some other way. A person who has never stated or expressed intent to cause harm may still pose a serious threat. In this case, the threat is usually detected because someone notices something unusual or troubling about the person's behavior, such as carrying weapons, stalking a target or decreased abilities to regulate and control their behavior. Similarly, just because a person has expressed intent to do harm does not necessarily mean that he/she poses a serious threat. It is the job of the TAM Team to gather relevant information and determine whether the person does, in fact, pose a threat — and if so, how best to intervene and reduce that threat.

## Principle 8:  Keep Victims in Mind

The TAM Team will need to pay attention to both victim safety and victim well-being. Victims are inherently more interested in threat management than threat assessment — meaning that they are more interested in what the Team will do to intervene, rather than what the particular assessment is. The TAM Team must often devote time and energy to managing victim or witness fears — at times, even when no significant threat may be posed. This is often the case if a violent episode has happened recently at another location. Persons who may be the target of violence may have some interest in the level of risk posed by the subject of concerns. However, nearly all such persons want the level of risk to be zero, regardless of what level an "expert" considers the risk to be. This encourages a focus on the management plan rather than focusing primarily on the level of risk.

---

49   Fein et al., 2002; Fein & Vossekuil, 1998; Fein, Vossekuil, & Holden (September 1995).
50   Fein et al., 2002; p. 33.

## Principle 9:  Early Identification and Intervention Helps Everyone

The emphasis of threat assessment and management is on the early recognition, reporting, and intervention with persons who have raised some concern. This guiding principle is directly related to the idea that targeted violence is frequently the end result of an identifiable pattern of thought and behavior.[51] The main task of the TAM Team is to recognize signs of these thoughts and behaviors that tend to precede violence, and to intervene as early as possible in order to prevent further escalation. In order to do that effectively, the TAM Team needs to learn about persons who have raised concern as early as possible. Volatile situations are like poured concrete — the longer they set, the harder they are to work with. The earlier a concern is recognized, the easier it is to address and resolve. Early identification also allows for a broader range of intervention options, especially those interventions that are less punitive or control oriented.

## Principle 10:
## Multiple Reporting Mechanisms Enhance Early Identification

In order to be effective, threat assessment and management requires simple and easy access to reporting, consultation and intervention resources. The TAM Team should make it as easy as possible for the campus community to report concerns and for the Team to quickly access the resources it needs in order to intervene appropriately. Having multiple means of reporting concerns — including anonymous tip lines, websites, and email addresses — as well as guidance on what to report, can all encourage campus community members to report concerns as early as possible. A multidisciplinary team better facilitates a multi-source, multi-method approach to early notification of problem situations. The broad representation of such a team provides more direct connections with a range of potential sources throughout the campus.

## Principle 11:
## Multi-Faceted Resources Can Provide Effective Interventions

When a TAM Team decides that it needs to intervene to reduce a threat, it will develop and implement a management plan. Threat management aims to utilize multiple, sustained, and coordinated interventions for maximum effectiveness.[52] Multiple strategies to de-escalate or contain the individual, connect the individual with the resources and assistance needed, reduce his/her access to the target, decrease the vulnerability of a potential target, and address situational or environmental factors

---

51   Fein et al., 2002; Vossekuil et al., 2002.
52   Fein et al., 2002.

should be used in concert in order to manage a threat. These efforts must often be sustained over periods of time, as the threat level in any particular case is likely to change.

## Principle 12: Safety Is a Primary Focus

Finally, the last guiding principle is that safety is the primary goal of all threat assessment and management efforts. The TAM Team's ultimate purpose is to ensure the safety of the campus community by identifying and managing threats. This goal must always be kept in mind, both in the short term through assessing and managing cases, and in the long run through outreach and training efforts. Any particular interventions — counseling, support, confrontation, termination, arrest, hospitalization, etc. — are tools to achieve the goals of safety. They are not ends unto themselves. For example, while a person's behavior may warrant expulsion or separation from the community, doing so may not, by itself, decrease the risk of the situation. It may, in fact, serve as a triggering event that inflames the person and precipitates progression along the pathway of violence. Therefore, the TAM Team must take additional measures to address broader safety concerns beyond what may be the institution's first inclination in how to handle a troublesome situation. This is not to suggest that institutions should fail to hold persons accountable for egregious behaviors — quite the contrary. Logical consequences of behavior, applied in a reasonable, fair and timely manner, generally serve to diminish escalation of adverse behaviors. However, the Team must remain cognizant of the possibility that such measures, however well intended or appropriate, may be perceived as a trigger for a volatile individual. Part of the Team's assessment and management plan should include planning for such a contingency.

# SECTION THREE

## TEAM COMPOSITION, ROLES AND RESPONSIBILITIES

# Team Composition, Roles and Responsibilities

### Team Composition

The Threat Assessment and Management Team is a multidisciplinary team composed of individuals from various departments on campus, thereby allowing for maximal collaboration and coordination of efforts. Having a multidisciplinary team means having representation from across an institution's various constituencies — administration, faculty, student life, and staff — and can also include departments such as buildings and grounds and/or food services, whose staff members are often in the position to see and hear things that faculty and administrators do not. Similarly, the Team can include representatives from local agencies and entities off campus that may have contact with students, faculty and staff outside of the institution. Examples include local law enforcement agencies, mental health services, and social services.

Even if a team does not include representatives from campus support staff or neighborhood entities, it should establish relationships with those departments and entities in order to let them know that the Team exists and wants reports from those departments, and to have a relationship in place if the Team needs to seek information from those departments or entities in a particular case. For example, campus maintenance and/or custodial staff may be in a position to see concerning items in a dorm room, such as weapons or pipe bomb components. If the TAM Team includes a representative from that department in its membership — or at least engages in periodic outreach to that department — the Team will be more likely to hear from the maintenance/custodial staff about the concerning items. Similarly, if the Team learns about a student and seeks information from the maintenance/custodial staff, the Team is more likely to get this information if the staff members are already aware of the Team's existence and its mission to increase everyone's safety. Having key support staff and local agency representatives on the Team can also help enhance the feeling among those departments and agencies that they play an important role in campus safety along with more traditional departments such as campus police.

A helpful way to think about Team membership and key liaison relationships is using the analogy of a sports team. The players are the most visible members of a sports team. These are analogous to the core

TAM Team members who meet, discuss, assess, manage and follow up. They are the ones who implement the plays and adjust to changing conditions or strategies on the field. However, the players are supported and enhanced by several other entities. The team owner provides strategic direction and authorization for the membership. This is akin to the institution's senior administration, which authorizes the mission and activities of the Team. A sports team has a coach who is knowledgeable and experienced in playing the game, sets general direction and guides the development of fundamental skills and the application of core principles. This is analogous to the team leader (discussed below) providing direction, structure and accountability for the TAM Team. Sports trainers provide for specific needs in support of players. Similarly, there are often subject matter experts on campus that may supplement the TAM Team's activities, but who are not directly involved in the assessment and on-going management of cases. One example may be environmental health or safety staff members who have expertise with a particular chemical that is referenced in a subject's threats. In addition, just as a sports team often has a marketing component that reminds people of its existence and generates interest, the TAM Team engages in community outreach efforts to advertise its existence and get the community involved. Finally, a sports team has scouts who search out new talent and monitor how other teams play and strategize. In a sense, these are all the members of the campus community, any of whom may be tapped to share information and observations that are relevant to a particular case. The Team, then, is not just those physically present around the table, but includes those who can contribute information or expertise to facilitate the most effective understanding and response.

---

*Decision Point*: **How large should your team be?**

The size of the TAM Team will be determined, in large part, by the Team's workload and the resources of the institution.[53] For example, a community college with several distinct campuses within a region may opt either to have one large team with representatives from each campus or smaller separate teams for each campus. Core team membership should be driven by the communication and working relationships that are necessary to achieve the mission of the Team. The institution can decide on the Team's initial membership, and then expand or contract as conditions dictate. A general guide is to have as few core members as are necessary to provide for a timely and objective review of cases. Having too many core members may make for difficult scheduling of regular meetings.

---

While each team is unique, we generally recommend that the TAM Team include representatives from the following departments or entities:[54]

- Academic Affairs / Provost
- Human Resource Services (for cases involving faculty or staff members)
- Media Relations
- Police / Security
- Residence Life (for colleges and universities with on-campus housing)
- Student Affairs / Dean of Students (for cases involving students)
- Mental health consultant
- Legal Counsel[55]
- Graduate and Professional Schools
- Specialty member (as determined on a case-by-case basis)

---

53  Calhoun & Weston, 2006.
54  The specific departments involved may vary depending upon whether the Team is handling a student case or a faculty/staff case.
55  Note: It is not necessary to have legal counsel participate in every meeting; but the team should at least meet with the institution's legal counsel periodically to discuss any concerns regarding information-sharing, record-keeping, and relevant disability law.

## Roles and Responsibilities

One individual on the TAM Team should be designated as the team leader. This individual will be responsible for running the Team meetings, assigning responsibilities to other team members, ensuring that the threat assessment and management process is followed, and leading and facilitating discussions. The team leader will also have authority for making decisions when the Team is divided on issues or in crisis situations. It is important that the leadership hierarchy on the Team be established, so that meetings can be run efficiently and goals are met with minimal time wasted in the process. In choosing the team leader, the TAM Team should select someone who relates well with others, has an inquisitive and skeptical mindset, and is familiar with threat assessment principles and practices. However, we do not recommend that the Team be led by the counseling center director or other counseling center staff, as this could put the team leader into a role conflict between facilitating information sharing in support of the TAM Team's work and maintaining patient confidentiality at the counseling center. In addition, the team leader should have the appropriate resources upon which to draw and have a good sense of judgment, objectivity, and thoroughness. Perhaps the most important quality for a team leader to possess is that she/he be passionate about the role and the work it entails.

In addition to the team leader, other individuals on the TAM Team have unique roles, responsibilities and resources — although all team members will be called upon at times to assist in gathering information from sources outside of their departments. Moreover, all available team members will participate in assessing the information gathered (as detailed in Section Four) and may also participate in developing, implementing, or monitoring a threat management plan. Some of the unique roles and responsibilities are as follows:[56]

> Academic Affairs / Provost: This team member acts as a liaison to/ from the college or university's academic units and centers, and is responsible for interpreting academic policies and priorities.

> Human Resource Services: This team member has access to employee information and records, and provides this information to the Team in cases where a faculty or staff member has raised some concern. He/she is responsible for interpreting personnel policies, contractual issues that may affect decision-making, and

---

56  Jaeger, L., Deisinger, E., Houghton, D., & Cychosz, C. (1993). *A coordinated response to critical incidents*. Ames, IA: Iowa State University.

generally acts as a liaison to/from Human Resources Services. This individual keeps the Team informed about important personnel developments, such as an anticipated termination of benefits or employment.

Media Relations: This individual is responsible for maintaining public information in major cases and relating it to the media when appropriate, and generally acts as a liaison to the media and the public. Even for internal cases, this member of the Team can provide valuable advice regarding how information about policies and procedures should be shared with the college/university community, as well as how information should be disseminated to the campus community regarding the operation of the Team. In addition, the Media Relations representative may be able to inform the Team about potential threats, such as those stemming from controversial research being conducted on campus.

Police / Security: If the college or university has its own police or security force, a representative of that unit should be on the Team. The police / security representative is responsible for conducting investigations and coordinating efforts with both internal and external law enforcement agencies. He/she coordinates emergency services and acts as a liaison for all law enforcement actions. An institution may also choose to involve representation from local law enforcement in addition to campus law enforcement or security services, or where there are no campus law enforcement or security services. In any case, the law enforcement or security department will be most effective when it maintains a strong focus on community policing and crime prevention.

Residence Life: Depending upon how much of the college or university's student population lives on campus in residential housing, it may be extremely helpful to have a Residence Life representative on the Team. If a significant portion of the student body lives on campus, then this representative will help the Team with detecting new cases, since Residence Life personnel may be aware of students who may be engaging in suspicious or concerning behavior in the on-campus dormitories or apartments. This team member can also be extremely valuable once a case is already under investigation by the Team because Residence Life personnel may be able to suggest which students know the person of concern and should be interviewed — and which should not.

Similarly, the Residence Life representative may have the ability to monitor individuals who may pose a threat and are being managed by the Team.

Student Affairs / Dean of Students: This person is responsible for interpreting the Student Code of Conduct and other student-related policies. This person also has access to student records and other information, provides this information to the Team, and acts as a liaison with students' parents and families. Other responsibilities include maintaining an up-to-date list of members of the TAM Team and serving as the liaison to administrative decision-makers.

Mental Health Consultant: This team member can provide helpful consultation regarding mental health issues and how they may impact upon a case. This person can come from the student counseling center, employee assistance program, or be an outside consultant. This person can also coordinate efforts with outside mental health agencies so that services are available to the individual who cannot be served adequately by campus services. No mental health professional that advises the Team should be in a treating relationship with anyone who is a focus of threat assessment or management efforts. This would likely result in a significant conflict of interest.

Legal Counsel: Legal counsel can provide guidance and advice regarding the development and operation of the Team to best ensure compliance with relevant laws and policies. The legal representative can also discuss privacy and confidentiality issues (see Section Six), facilitate obtaining court injunctions and Temporary Restraining Orders, and assist in preparing legal documents to deal with potentially dangerous situations.

Graduate and Professional Schools: If the college or university has a graduate and/or professional schools, it is particularly important to have a representative of the graduate / professional schools on the Team in addition to the Undergraduate Dean of Students. Some teams find that a greater proportion of graduate students — compared with undergraduate students — is reported to the Team. A representative from the graduate / professional school may be able to inform the Team about dynamics that are unique to, or more pronounced for, graduate students — such as pressure to achieve academic goals, reliance on the approval of one or two faculty members for advancement (rather than on passing grades in coursework), and added dynamics such as cultural influences for foreign graduate students.

Specialty Member: In addition to the regular members who comprise the Team, it may also be helpful, on a case by case basis, to include a specialty member(s). This may include someone who knows the student or employee in question, so that he/she can provide an inside perspective and assist with the Team's assessment and management of the case.[57] It may also include someone from a department on campus that can provide case-specific information. For example, a member of Religious Life may be helpful for cases where religion may be important to the person; a member of the Chemistry department may be helpful in cases where chemicals have been found in a student's dorm room; or a member from the student gay, lesbian, bisexual, and transgender organization may be helpful in cases where hazing of a gay student is involved.

Each member of the TAM Team has his/her own area of expertise, and makes a unique contribution to the Team. It is important that team members not overstep their area of expertise when giving input and making recommendations. When decisions are made or information is provided, it should generally be done by the individual who is an expert in that particular area. For example, the Media Relations representative should not provide input about mental health issues when he/she has no demonstrated or recognized expertise in that field. Rather, only the mental health professionals should advise the Team on how any such issues affect the case. Similarly, the mental health professionals should not be the primary voice about issues for which they have no recognized expertise (e.g., student disciplinary or Human Resources regulations).

However, team members should be encouraged to question each other and to raise any and all observations or concerns as they relate to the case in question or the team's process. In addition, situations may arise in which no one on the TAM Team is qualified to make expert opinions. In such cases, we encourage the Team to consult with outside experts or threat assessment and management teams at other institutions, if time permits.

---

57  Jaeger et al., 1993.

The members of the TAM Team should be trained as a team so that they learn how to work well together and how the threat assessment and management process works.[58] Team training exercises not only provide the TAM Team with experience in how to respond in various "What if" scenarios, but they also provide an excellent opportunity for relationship building among the team members. Section Seven provides more information on the types of training recommended.

---

### *Who is qualified to be on a TAM Team?*

Campus representatives who serve on the TAM Team must clearly have the knowledge, skills, and abilities necessary to be effective in their primary positions. However, they must also be able to utilize those skills to maximize the effectiveness of the Team. Although no particular team member will likely meet all of the following criteria, the team members should be able to ***collectively*** demonstrate the skills and abilities listed below:

- Commitment to the safety of the campus community.
- Commitment to fair, objective, reasonable and timely efforts to enhance safety.
- Ability to recognize situations that may pose a concern to the safety, well-being, or effective operation of the campus community.
- Ability to demonstrate sensitivity to a wide variety of issues and diversity of persons involved.
- Ability to be flexible and open to creative problem-solving approaches.
- Ability and willingness to share information lawfully and appropriately.
- Ability to gather, organize, and interpret complex information from multiple sources.
- Ability to analyze problems and complaints by synthesizing information and observing behavior.
- Knowledge of threat assessment, intervention, management, and communication techniques and procedures. (This can be achieved through training for the Team or for individual team members.)

---

58　Fein et al., 2002.

- Ability to communicate effectively with difficult employees, students or others.
- Ability to consult with employees and organizations to develop plans and strategies to alleviate problems.
- Ability to document, prepare, update, and maintain confidential records.
- Knowledge of college and university policies and procedures related to violence and campus safety.
- Knowledge of state and federal laws related to privacy and confidentiality.
- Knowledge of personnel and labor law issues, sufficient to advise management.
- Ability to communicate and effectively present information (verbally and in writing) to a wide range of audiences, including senior administration, faculty, staff and students.
- Ability to recognize the limits of their professional knowledge and skills.
- Openness to seek out consultation when necessary.
- Ability to work independently to complete designated responsibilities.
- Ability to handle crisis communications.
- Knowledge of community resources, such as social services and mental health professionals.
- Ability to make critical decisions, assessments and recommendations.
- Commitment to follow-up and resolution of situations.

# SECTION FOUR

## THE THREAT ASSESSMENT AND MANAGEMENT PROCESS

# The Threat Assessment and Management Process

When a campus TAM Team first learns about a threat or other concerning behavior, there is a general sequence of steps the Team can take to screen the case, determine whether to initiate a team-led inquiry, gather information, evaluate the person and situation involved, and develop and implement a management strategy where necessary.

It is important to note that there are several ways to accomplish these steps, and that they do not necessarily need to be taken in the order in which they are presented here. For instance, the steps can be taken sequentially, or they can be divided up by the team members and tackled concurrently. The Team can also address later components earlier in the process, depending on the Team's best judgment. Finally, information gathered in the inquiry process should be fed back to the Team as it is gathered — both to keep team members current with information as it is gathered, and because new information may alter the direction of the inquiry or suggest other areas to explore.

The major steps of the campus threat assessment and management process are as follows:[59]

1.  **Identify a student, faculty member, or staff member who has engaged in threatening behaviors or done something that raised serious concern about their well-being, stability, or potential for violence or suicide.**[60]

In order for the Team to learn about persons who have threatened or seriously concerned other people, those on campus (i.e., faculty, staff, students, others) must know that there is a process for handling such concerns and that they should report threats and troubling/worrisome behavior to the Team. Even if campus personnel and students do not report their concerns to the Team, they should report them to someone on campus that they trust (e.g., a supervisor, residential advisor, faculty member, counseling center staff, etc.) and those officials should know to pass that information on to the Team. Referrals to the Team can also

59  These steps are based on Fein et al. (2002), Calhoun & Weston (2003) and Mohandie (2000) and the consulting experience of the primary authors, and have been adapted for a higher education environment.

60  Fein et al., 2002; Calhoun & Weston (2003).

come from established disciplinary and security entities on campus and in the community, such as judicial affairs, human resources, campus security, and local law enforcement.

### Encouraging Reporting

Identification depends, in large part, upon the willingness and ability of the campus community to communicate with the TAM Team and make the Team aware of any concerns or suspicions they may have about a particular individual's behavior. Therefore, a critical element of this first step is to encourage the campus community to look for warning signs and report them. All too often, people are only willing to come forward with their concerns about an individual following a violent episode elsewhere. For example, following the Virginia Tech shootings, members of campus communities throughout the country suddenly became much more aware of the behavior of others around them and more willing to report them out of fear that they might be the next campus shooter. This fear, however, will not last long. Therefore, the college or university must make a consistent effort to remind the campus community that reports about suspicious behavior are wanted, what signs to look for, how to report them, and that their concerns will be taken seriously and investigated objectively.

What information is reported from established entities on campus will depend on instructions from the TAM Team, institutional policy, and/ or the institution's leadership. We recommend that judicial affairs and campus security report any repeat offenders, or any behavior that seems out of the ordinary or otherwise "worrisome." What information is reported from faculty, staff, and students on campus will depend on how the campus is educated about reporting. We recommend that campus students and personnel be encouraged to report any threats and any other behavior that they find troubling or upsetting; the message should be that there is no penalty for reporting, and that the Team wants to hear about behavior that causes some worry or concern, even if the behavior seems low-level or unclear. It is also important to emphasize that the Team's efforts are oriented around assistance, not primarily (or solely) punitive actions.

We recommend a multi-pronged approach. First, the Team should provide general awareness training and/or information for the entire campus (and select community members who have regular contact with students and/ or faculty and staff). The awareness training should let the campus know that the Team exists; emphasize that the Team is there for everyone's help and safety; underscore that for persons referred to the Team, most of what is done gets those persons connected with assistance that they need; provide a broad view of the types of concerns the Team wants to know about; and give clear instructions on how to report information to the Team. The awareness training should be held at least once a year, and can be part of another campus-wide event such as convocation, annual distribution of Clery notices (see box on Campus Outreach below), online training and information, and in-person training and awareness sessions.

Second, the Team should provide multiple ways that students, faculty, staff, and others (e.g. parents) can report information — including to their Residential Advisors (RAs), to a professor, to an anonymous tip line and website, etc. Remind the campus often about what and how to report through emails, banners on the institution's website, Public Service Announcements on the college radio station, and signs around campus that encourage community members to report safety concerns, i.e., "If you see something, say something."[61]

Third, the Team should provide periodic notification to parents to let them know that the Team exists for their student's safety, and encourage parents to talk with the Team if they have any concerns about their own son or daughter, or another person on campus. Many campuses have well-developed admissions and orientation programs for parents to inform them about a myriad of campus resources.

---

### Campus Outreach

The TAM Team has many options for how it can reach out to the entire campus community in order to encourage reporting. Effective techniques include running an ad in the school newspaper or putting up posters throughout campus, particularly in central locations where community members are likely to gather. Information should be posted on the institution's website, including links to the college or university's anti-violence policy and procedures. Staff and student orientation provides an excellent outreach opportunity. In addition, since every institution of higher education is already required to report its crime statistics annually under the Campus Security Act (also known as the Clery Act), the TAM Team can capitalize on this reporting by making this and other safety-related information known to the entire community through the release of a yearly bulletin that can be printed and distributed in hard copies or delivered electronically via email.

---

61  State of New York Metropolitan Transportation Authority, available at *http://www.mta.info/ mta/security/index.html*, retrieved October 29, 2008.

When a team is newly formed and needs to prioritize its initial outreach efforts, it should focus its initial outreach on campus offices where problems are likely to already exist. These "touch points" include places on campus where decisions with consequences are made — such as changes in a student's enrollment status, denial of financial aid, or termination of employee benefits. Such locations might include (but are not limited to) key administrator offices, the President's office, the Provost's office, the Dean of Students' office, the judicial office, the Financial Aid or Treasurer's office, and Human Resources. Such training should be designed not only to assist key administrators in recognizing, de-escalating and better managing situations of concern, but also to help support staff better recognize and deal with such situations. Administrative support staff members often have opportunity to observe and interact with persons of concern while those persons are waiting for their appointments with administrators. Support staff members feel more confident and empowered to deal with such situations when provided adequate training and support.

Training should also be provided to students, particularly Resident Advisors (RAs). These students have a unique opportunity to monitor their peers' behavior where they reside. By training RAs about how to recognize troubling signs, such as drug/alcohol abuse or not leaving one's dormitory room for long periods of time, the TAM Team increases the likelihood of an early intervention.

### Checking In Around Campus

Even if departments such as judicial affairs or campus police do not actively submit reports to the Team, they can still be contacted to see if they are aware of any concerning students, faculty, or staff members. The Team can do simple liaison or outreach activities to those departments to encourage them to report and to check in with them periodically (e.g., weekly, bi-monthly, monthly) to see if any persons have come on their radar screen for troubling or worrisome behavior. Departments where the Team can (and should) "check in" include the following:

- **Student judicial process** - Nearly all campuses have student conduct standards and related judicial procedures for violations of those standards. TAM Teams should have connections with representatives from the student judicial process in order to remain informed about students demonstrating severe behavior (or patterns of behavior) of concern — and to be able to make a quick inquiry when a student is reported to the Team for a threat or other troubling behavior.

- **Faculty grievance/conduct boards** - Many campuses have faculty conduct standards and related review committees and procedures. Again, TAM Teams should have connections with board representatives to monitor patterns of behavior that demonstrate concern.

- **Staff grievance review committees** - Staff with patterns of unfounded, unreasonable or un-resolvable grievances may be appropriate subjects for threat assessment review.

- **Equal opportunity & diversity offices** - Most campuses have an office designated for receiving complaints of harassment and discrimination. Chronic, frequent, unsubstantiated complaints may indicate a need for threat assessment review.

- **University legal counsel** - Legal counsel may be aware of civil actions or major disciplinary proceedings.

- **Campus police or security departments** - Campus (and local) police, as well as campus security departments, may have contacts with persons whose behavior does not result in criminal charges, but which may reflect violations of conduct standards or indicate a need for assistance. Campus police may also run checks regarding criminal history, weapons, and sex-offender registration. In situations where a subject of concern has come from another community or institution, campus police are often more able (than a non-law enforcement member of the Team) to obtain information from the law enforcement agencies at those previous locations. This may include law enforcement contacts that did not result in arrest and therefore would not appear in a criminal history.

- **Local law enforcement** - The Team should establish a relationship with local law enforcement even if there is a campus police department or campus security department. The relationship can be initiated by the campus police/security representative to the TAM Team but can also be done through the team's leader. It is quite possible that a student, faculty member, or staff member may be arrested by the local police without campus ever being notified about it. Having that relationship in advance will encourage local police to volunteer information to the Team — but a regular and timely check-in with the local police department can also facilitate that information-sharing.

Reports from campus and local police or security departments can be very good sources of information about potential concerns. This includes review of incidents of criminal activity (e.g., harassment, stalking, etc.) as well as responses to persons exhibiting suspicious (but non-criminal behavior), health and welfare visits, and medical situations (some of which may reflect suicidality, severe mental health issues, or substance abuse).

Depending on state law and agency policy, police may be limited in providing their actual criminal investigative or intelligence reports. However, they can usually share pertinent information with persons having a need to know.

Beyond investigative reports, security and law enforcement agencies may have other public records such as dispatch/calls for service records that document the initial information received by the agency. This is often public information. They will also have the finding and disposition of each of those calls. Many departments have internal master name indices through which they can track contacts with persons in any capacity (e.g., as victims, suspects, witnesses, intelligence sources, etc.).

- **Residential Life conduct boards** - Some institutions have Residential Life staff members who deal with conduct issues that occur within university housing. Residence life staff (both professional and student staff) may have observations or knowledge about inappropriate behaviors that did not result in formal proceedings.

- **Honor boards** - A relatively small number of institutions have honor codes and associated review processes. Persons who demonstrate persistent difficulty in abiding by the expectations of such codes may be appropriate for threat assessment review.

- **Greek Council/fraternity and sorority system (or other student social organizations that may or may not be formally linked to campus)** - These organizations will have a perspective on students (although likely not staff or faculty) that may differ from the perspective of those students in the classroom or at campus locations like the dining hall or library. Liaison with these organizations should emphasize that the Team can be a resource to those student organizations to help them manage difficult behavior or members. Framing the relationship in terms of what the Team can do to help the organizations may facilitate them volunteering or sharing information more so than an approach where they feel they are being asked to "turn in" their members and friends.

- **Community entities such as hospitals** - In addition, we recommend establishing relationships with other community groups or entities that have periodic or regular contact with students, faculty, and/or staff. Examples include local hospitals (e.g., the counseling center director can establish a liaison with the local hospital's psychiatric staff; the head of the campus health center can establish a liaison with the hospital's emergency room staff; etc.), establishments that employ a large number of students, and community groups such as Big Brothers/Big Sisters.

## 2.   Conduct an initial screening.

When the TAM Team first learns about a person who has acted in a threatening way or otherwise raised concern, the Team should conduct an initial screening to determine — first and foremost — whether there is an imminent danger or emergency situation.

If there is an emergency situation or imminent danger, the team leader or some other member of the Team should immediately contact campus law enforcement/security (or local law enforcement, for campuses without a campus law enforcement presence).

Before any situations arise, the Team should first discuss with campus administrators, campus law enforcement, and/or local law enforcement what situations would constitute an "emergency" or "imminent situation." For example, a team might turn a situation over immediately to law enforcement for response and investigation when a subject has a weapon, has indicated a threat to use it, and appears ready to act on an opportunity to do so. Such a situation should be viewed as an imminent danger and should generally be turned over to law enforcement immediately.

Determining whether there is an imminent danger will generally be based on the information that is reported to the Team and any other information the Team already possesses. This is because a potentially imminent situation may allow minimal time for information-gathering, and instead require a quick response to contain the person in question.

If the situation appears to be urgent or an imminent threat, then steps should be taken immediately to contain the person, effect an arrest, or possibly get the subject to an emergency psychiatric evaluation if the circumstances allow — rather than focusing on a detailed threat assessment inquiry at that time.

In such a situation, a full inquiry should be launched either once the person is contained or concurrently with law enforcement efforts to contain the person. The rationale for doing a full inquiry in an imminent situation comes from the fact that once the urgency of the situation has passed, the person will be released at some point and may then pose a threat to the campus community. It is therefore still important for the Team to determine whether the person poses a threat or otherwise needs intervention, and if so, to develop and implement a plan to reduce the threat and intervene with appropriate support to help address the person's long-term problems.

If the Team determines that there is not an emergency or imminent situation at hand, the next thing it needs to do is determine whether there is a need for a full inquiry. To do this, the Team should begin by gathering initial information from several key sources, including:

- A review of previous contacts made through the threat assessment or assistance process, sometimes referred to as "pinging the system" (see Section Six);

- Student Affairs (for a case involving a student) or Human Resources (for a case involving a faculty member or staff member);

- Campus police/security and local law enforcement (even in cases where there is a campus law enforcement department, both the campus and local departments should be contacted; campus law enforcement can also act as liaison to the surrounding community's police department in these cases and request information on behalf of the Team);

- Academic affairs (if the case involves a student);

- Residential staff (for a case involving a student); and

- An online search of the person's name, the name of the institution, and the name(s) of anyone they may have threatened, harassed, pursued, or scared. Recommended websites to search include:

  o Google.com

  o MySpace.com

  o Facebook.com

  o YouTube.com

  o Cuil.com

  o Technorati.com (searches blogs)

  o Twitter.com

  o *Blackplanet.com*

  o *MiGente.com*

   o *Bebo.com*

   o *Xanga.com*

   o *Craigslist.com* (search the relevant city/town)

   o *Thehoodup.com*

   o *JuicyCampus.com*

The Team can then use this preliminary information to answer some triage questions, in order to determine whether a full inquiry is warranted. Those triage questions include:

1. Has there been any mention of suicidal thoughts, plans, or attempts?

2. Has there been any mention of thoughts/plans of violence?

3. Have there been any behaviors that cause concern for violence or the person's well-being?

4. Does the person have access to a weapon or are they trying to gain access?

5. Are there behaviors that are significantly disruptive to the campus environment?

If there is a "yes" response to any of these questions, a full inquiry is recommended, as this may indicate an imminent risk as well as a need for further assessment. However, the initial priority is on managing and controlling the acute situation. As that control is effected, the Team can continue to evaluate and manage any on-going threat posed by the situation.

If there is any suggestion that the person has broken the law, then an investigation (run by law enforcement rather than the Team) may be initiated — but the Team should first consider whether handing the situation over to campus or law enforcement at that time might have an adverse impact on the safety of the situation in question and possibly increase the person's risk for violence or suicide. For example, in some circumstances when law enforcement is notified of a situation, they must arrest the person in question, and this may make the individual more volatile and dangerous upon his/her release. The Team should also consider whether handing the case over to law enforcement at that time may reduce the options the institution has available for managing the person and reducing the risk. The case can always be turned over to law enforcement at a later point.

If the answer to all five questions is "no" AND the Team gathered sufficient information to be able to answer those questions fully (i.e., no further information is needed in order to answer the questions completely), then no further inquiry is necessary. However, the incident that brought the person to the Team's attention should still be entered into the Team's case database (see Section Six) and the results of the initial inquiry should be documented and kept, in case the person comes back to the Team's attention at a later date and still has assistance needs.

## 3.　Conduct a full inquiry.[62]

If a full inquiry is necessary, the Team should add to the information already gathered by first identifying who in the person's life may have some information the Team needs to know. Prior to most campus, school, and workplace attacks, there was considerable information available about the attacker's violent ideas and plans, as well as information that the attacker was already concerning several people. But this information was scattered among several different sources.[63] Faculty members had noticed something troubling, family members knew other troubling facts, fellow students or colleagues had heard threats or mentions of ideas and plans of violence, and Internet posts showed other details about potential harm. The role of the Team in a threat assessment inquiry is to figure out who might have a piece of the puzzle, ask those people what they know about the person in question, and then assemble all of those pieces of the puzzle to determine whether the person poses a threat or otherwise needs help or intervention.

The questioning should be conducted cautiously so as not to unduly compromise the privacy of the persons involved or to raise concerns among witnesses who are interviewed. The questioning does not have to be complicated. It need only be along the lines of asking if they have noticed, heard, or been told anything about the person that seems out of the ordinary, troubling, or concerning. People may naturally not want to "overreact" or "sound the alarm" if they are concerned that what they have noticed is really nothing. The Team's job is to overcome that natural reluctance by encouraging them to share any and every observation they have had, even if they preface what they tell the Team with "This may be nothing, but...." The Team should emphasize that it is attempting to develop the most complete understanding of the situation that is possible. Team members may also emphasize that the primary purpose of the Team's involvement is to address safety concerns, and (where possible) to assist the individual in question, rather than punish him or her.

---

62　Calhoun & Weston, 2003; Fein et al., 2002; Mohandie, 2000.
63　Vossekuil et al., 2002.

*Gathering Information*

The following is a list of departments and other sources from which the Team may wish to solicit additional information about the person in question. This list is similar to the list of departments where the TAM Team should check in on a regular basis; however, the focus at this point is on what (if any) information these entities may have about the *particular* person who is the subject of a full inquiry.

- **Faculty and staff members** - All campus faculty and staff members are potential sources of information about someone on campus who has raised concern(s). It is important to think broadly about staff who may know the person — in particular, support staff from departments such as buildings & grounds, food services, and other staff who may be in a position to observe behavior, offices, and dorm rooms, even if they do not have direct contact with or know the person directly. One K-12 shooting was stopped because a janitor found a note on the floor detailing plans for a school attack and knew to bring the note to the TAM Team. Some persons of concerns may confide in support staff because they are not in a position of authority; others may engage in behavior in front of support staff without knowing or caring they are there because they consider such staff as "invisible." Either way, those staff members may hold critical pieces of information.

- **Student judicial process** - Whenever a student is reported to the TAM Team because they did something that raised concern, their judicial history should be check for prior contacts, patterns of problems, and escalation of rule-breaking behavior, as well as any existing support or control measures that may remain under judicial control. It is also important to determine if there are any pending disciplinary actions that may be escalating the student's reactivity or that may negatively impact upon the student's academic status.

- **Faculty grievance/conduct boards** - If a faculty member has been referred to the TAM Team, the Team should check with the conduct or grievance board to see if the person is known to the board for any reason or has any pending actions that may be relevant. A history of grievances or inappropriate conduct may enhance understanding of the current situation.

- **Staff grievance review committees** - If a staff member has been referred to the TAM Team, the Team should check with the staff grievance committee to see if the person is known to the board for any reason or has pending grievances.

- **Equal opportunity & diversity offices** - For faculty and staff cases, the Team should check with these departments to see if they know of the person for significant, chronic, frequent, and/or unsubstantiated claims of discrimination, sexual harassment or other prejudices.

- **University legal counsel** -Legal counsel should be queried to see if they are aware of any information about the person in question that may stem from civil cases against the university or other proceedings in which counsel have been consulted.

- **Campus police or security departments** - Campus police, as well as campus security departments, can be queried to see if the person has come to their attention for violations of conduct standards or behavioral problems that fall short of criminal charges, as well as for criminal violations. They can also be asked to run weapons checks, or this can be done through the local law enforcement agency. An inquiry of any contacts police have had with the subject may provide information about habits or potential focus on targets (e.g., parking violations).

- **Residential Life conduct boards** - For cases involving students, residence life staff (both professional and student staff) can be asked about the student of concern. Residential life staff may have observations or knowledge about inappropriate behaviors that did not result in formal proceedings. They also may be aware of escalations of behavior or deterioration in personal hygiene or conduct that indicates concern. Discussions with student residence life staff — as with any other students — should be conducted with discretion and with the ultimate message that the Team's interest is to help the student in question as well as to maintain campus safety.

- **Honor boards** - An institution's honor board, if there is one, can be asked whether the student in question has shown difficulty in abiding by the expectations of the institution's codes or has shown other behavioral problems that impact their ability to adhere to institutional rules.

- **Greek Council/fraternity and sorority system (or other student social organizations that may or may not be formally linked to campus)** - These organizations may have a perspective on a student of concern that may differ from the perspective of that student in the classroom or at campus locations like the dining hall or library. Similar to talking with residence life staff, leadership within the Greek system or a particular fraternity or sorority can be queried about a particular student, with discretion and with the message that the Team's interest is designed to get the student help as well as to prevent harm.

- **Local law enforcement** - We recommend that in addition to campus law enforcement or security, local law enforcement also be contacted anytime the Team initiates a full inquiry into a student, faculty member, or staff member. Contact with local law enforcement can be made through campus law enforcement or campus security, as that may make the information-sharing process easier. Local law enforcement may be aware of arrests or contact with the person in question, even if the contact never came to the attention of the institution. Again, the focus here is on understanding known behavior, whether or not it resulted in criminal charges or convictions. While a criminal history check can sometimes be helpful, it should not be assumed to be a complete or sufficient review of prior "bad acts."

- **Previous schools / employers** - In the case of a student, the Team can request information from the student's prior institutions, including high school and any previously-attended colleges or graduate schools (in the case of a graduate student). With caution and discretion, the Team can also inquire of the student's previous employers, especially in the case of non-traditional-age students.

  Depending on the circumstances, the Team may also decide to contact the person's family — including spouse or significant other for older students, as well as parents for younger students or older students still living with (or recently living with) their parents — if, in the Team's estimation, doing so would not aggravate the situation for the person of concern.

  In the case of a faculty or staff member, similar queries can be run — including prior employers and family members and/or significant others. For any interviews with family members/parents/spouses, it is important to keep in mind that such individuals may be very motivated NOT to see their family member/spouse/child as capable of violence or suicide. Therefore, information from these sources should be corroborated with information from other sources.

- **Email / Internet information** - Depending upon the institution's policies, the TAM Team may be able to access the email account and Internet search histories of the person in question. Email correspondence and Internet searches can provide critical information about the person's interests, ideas, or intent on violence and/or suicide. An institution that clearly articulates to campus personnel and students that it is allowed to access any institution's email accounts and/or Internet traffic in emergency situations may be able to provide the Team with access to this information in a particular case.

- **Health / Counseling Center** - While federal regulations and state laws generally prohibit counseling medical staff from sharing patient information with the TAM Team without the patient's permission, there are certain circumstances under which these prohibitions do not apply (see Section Six for a more detailed discussion of the Health Insurance Portability and Accountability Act and the Family Educational Rights and Privacy Act). Therefore, it is important that the Team be familiar with these laws and regulations and the conditions under which information can legally be obtained. In addition, it is important to keep in mind that while it may not always be possible to receive information *from* mental health professionals, there are ways to share information _with_ counseling or health center staff that do not violate federal regulations or state mental health laws.

- **Person of Concern** - Depending on the circumstances and the Team's judgment, the Team may decide to interview the person in question as part of the inquiry. In fact, doing so can serve as a preventative measure because it will give the person a chance to tell his/her side of the story. The opportunity to be heard can be effective in reducing anger and hostility. Interviewing can also provide an opportunity to establish some rapport or an alliance with the person in question, which will be helpful if the Team needs to intervene with the person through a management plan.

The TAM Team should discuss who is best suited to engage with, interview and intervene with the subject of concern. In situations where the subject appears volatile and exhibits high-risk behaviors, such an approach is often best handled by law enforcement or security professionals who are trained in interviewing techniques, and who are effective in assessing and de-escalating subjects in the field. It is often helpful to conduct such interviews at the subject's residence, both to facilitate more privacy, as well as to provide an opportunity to directly assess their living conditions or evidence of planning or preparation for violence.

For lower risk situations, the interviews may be better conducted by other team members (e.g., Dean of Students or Human Resources staff) or persons who have a connection with the subject. This may be less threatening to the subject than being approached by a law enforcement officer.

## 4. Answer key inquiry questions.[64]

Once the Team has gathered information about the person in question and his/her current situation, the next step is to then sort through the information to see what comprehensive picture of the person emerges. It is important to note that this threat assessment differs from a mental health risk assessment, which focuses primarily on the risk for impulsive violence rather than on the predatory violence seen in campus, workplace, and school attacks. Mental health risk assessment can be a highly useful tool as part of an individualized case management tool (see Step 6 below) but should not replace the threat assessment steps outlined here.

Once the Team has gathered, organized, and documented the information it has collected in Step 3, we recommend that the Team first use this information to answer several key inquiry questions.[65] These questions are designed to help organize the information gathered, as well as to use these facts to answer the ultimate inquiry questions as to whether the person in question poses a threat — and if not, whether the person still may be in need of a referral to resources that can help them.

### a. What are the person's motive(s) and goals?

- What motivated the person to make the statements or take the actions that caused him or her to come to the Team's attention?
- Does the situation or circumstance that led to these statements or actions still exist?
- Does the person have a major grievance or grudge? If so, against whom or what?
- What efforts have been made to resolve the problem and what has been the result?
- Does the person feel that any part of the problem is resolved or see any alternatives?

---

64  Fein et al., 2002.

65  These questions are taken largely from Fein et al. (2002) and have been modified for a higher education setting and to be used for faculty and staff who raise some concern, as well as for students. The guidance for how to weigh or interpret responses to the questions has been provided by the authors.

- Has the person expressed any justifications for violence?
- Has the person indicated lack of concern for any consequences of violent or inappropriate behavior?

The purpose of this question, and its sub-questions, is to understand the overall context of the behavior that first brought the person to the attention of the TAM Team, and also to understand whether those conditions or situation still exists. If those conditions still exist, the Team can use that information in crafting a management or referral/monitoring plan if necessary.

For example, if a student is reported to the Team because she wrote a violent essay for a class assignment, the Team can ask what the class assignment was. If the assignment was to write a graphic, scary, or controversial story — and the Team uncovers no other concerning information about the student — it is likely that the student in question was only following the professor's instructions and does not pose a threat.

**b.** *Have there been any communications suggesting ideas or intent to attack?*

- What, if anything, has the person communicated to someone else (e.g., targets, friends, co-workers, faculty, family, others) or written in a diary, journal, email, or website concerning his or her grievances, ideas and/or intentions?
- Have friends been alerted or "warned away"?

If the Team finds that the person in question has communicated an idea or plan to do harm — and that the source of that information is credible (i.e., it was not reported by someone trying to get the person in trouble) — this is a strong indication that the person may be on a pathway toward violence and therefore poses a threat. The Team should try to confirm or corroborate this information through another source, or through other information about the person's behavior that confirms an idea or plan to do harm.

**c.** *Has the person shown inappropriate interest in any of the following?*

- Workplace, school or campus attacks or attackers;
- Weapons (including recent acquisition of any relevant weapon);
- Incidents of mass violence (terrorism, workplace violence, mass murderers);

- Obsessive pursuit, stalking or monitoring others.

A "yes" to this question alone does not necessarily indicate that the person in question poses a threat or is otherwise in need of some assistance. Many people are interested in these topics but never pose any threat. However, if a person shows some fascination or fixation on any of these topics and has raised concern in another way, such as by expressing an idea to do harm to others or to himself/herself, recently purchasing a weapon, or showing helplessness or despair, the combination of these facts should increase the Team's concern about the person in question.

d. **Has the person engaged in attack-related behaviors (i.e., any behavior that moves an idea of harm forward toward actual harm)?** These behaviors might include:

- Developing an attack idea or plan;
- Making efforts to acquire or practice with weapons or other material to support an attack;
- Surveilling possible sites and areas for attack;
- Stalking or surveilling potential targets;
- Testing access to potential targets;
- Rehearsing attacks or ambushes.

If the Team determines that the person has engaged in any attack-related behavior, this is an indication that the person is on a pathway toward violence and has taken a step(s) forward toward carrying out an idea to do harm. Any of these behaviors should prompt the Team to try to corroborate or confirm these behaviors through other sources (or confirm the reliability of the source reporting these behaviors). These behaviors will give the Team an indication of how far along the pathway of violence the person has progressed, and may also help the Team understand how quickly the person is moving forward toward an attack — i.e., how imminent a threat there may be. Any attack-related behaviors should be seen as a serious indication of potential violence.

e. **Does the person have the capacity to carry out an act of targeted violence?**

- How organized is the person's thinking and behavior?
- Does the person demonstrate ability to act on thoughts?
- Does the person have the means (e.g., access to a weapon) to carry out an attack?

It is important for the Team to ask whether the person in question has access to weapons and ammunition. A "yes" to this question may be cause for concern. However, it is important for the Team to recognize that in some areas of the country, it is quite common to own weapons and to have experience using weapons from a young age. Therefore, what the Team should focus on is the combination of the person owning or having access to weapons AND some indication that the person has an idea or plan to do harm. Similarly, the Team should be concerned if the person develops an idea to do harm and THEN starts showing an interest in weapons. Either combination should raise the Team's concern, and move the Team toward determining that the person poses a threat.

### f.   Is the person experiencing hopelessness, desperation and/or despair?

- Is there information to suggest that the person is experiencing desperation and/or despair?
- Has the person experienced a recent failure or loss (including loss of status)?
- Is the person known to be having difficulty coping with a stressful event?
- Has the person engaged in behavior that suggests that he or she has considered committing suicide?

Many persons who have engaged in targeted violence have been suicidal prior to their attacks or actively suicidal at the time of their attacks, hoping to kill themselves or be killed by responding police. It is important to emphasize that most people who are feeling hopeless, desperate, or even suicidal will not pose a threat of harm to others. However, these people are still in need of help, possibly involving a quick referral for help. If the Team determines that the person in question is experiencing — or has recently experienced — desperation, hopelessness, and/or thoughts of suicide and there is NO other information indicating the person has thoughts or plans to harm other people, the Team should develop a plan to refer the person to necessary mental health care or emergency psychiatric intervention, possibly involving the institution's counseling center and/or police or local law enforcement if necessary. If the Team determines that the person in question is experiencing — or has recently experienced — desperation, hopelessness, and/or thoughts of suicide and there IS information that the person also has thoughts or plans to harm other people, the Team should determine that the person poses a threat and move to develop and implement a management plan to intervene with the person. The management plan should include resources to evaluate and treat the person's desperation and/or suicidal thoughts/plans.

g. **Does the person have a trusting relationship with at least one responsible person (e.g., a friend, significant other, roommate, colleague, faculty advisor, coach, parent, etc.)?**

- Does the person have at least one person he or she can confide in — someone the person believes will listen without judging or jumping to conclusions?
- Is the person emotionally connected to other people?

A "yes" to this question is good news. First, having someone that the person in question already trusts may be a protective factor in itself. This means that the responsible person may already be a good influence on the person. But more importantly, if the Team decides that the person in question poses a threat of harm, the Team can solicit the help of this responsible person. For example, this person can assist in developing a management plan, can work with the person who has raised concern, and can be used as a vehicle to get the person of concern to necessary help. The responsible person can also be encouraged to take a more active role in discouraging the person of concern from engaging in any harm — whether to himself/herself, others, or both.

h. **Does the person see violence as an acceptable, desirable, or only way to solve problems?**

- Does the person's social network(s) (e.g., friends, co-workers, students, parents, faculty members, colleagues, etc.) explicitly or implicitly support or endorse violence as a way of resolving problems or disputes?
- Does the person identify with perpetrators of violence?
- Does the person glorify acts of violence?
- Has the person been "dared" by others to engage in an act of violence?
- Has the person communicated a lack of perceived alternatives to violence or a persistence and resentful sense of powerlessness?

If the Team learns that the person in question sees violence as a potential, reasonable, desirable, or even the only solution to their problems, it will give the Team some indication of the person's inclination toward violence. More importantly, it can indicate how much of an adverse impact the person's problem or current situation may be having on them. Therefore, a "yes" to this question should increase the Team's concern about the person in question. But it should also lead the Team to consider what options they may have for helping the person solve their problems or improve their situation so that the person no longer looks toward violence as a solution.

### i.   Is the person's conversation and "story" consistent with his or her actions?

- Does information from collateral interviews and from the person's own behavior confirm or dispute what the person of concern says is going on?
- Does information from an interview with the person of concern lead the Team to believe the person's account of his or her situation? How trustworthy is the person in interactions with the Team?

If the TAM Team decides to interview the person of concern, the interview can be used as an opportunity to determine how forthcoming or truthful the person is being with the Team. The less forthcoming the person is, the more work the Team may have to do to develop an alliance if a management plan is needed.

### j.   Are other people concerned about the person's potential for violence?

- Are those who know the person concerned that he or she might take action based on violent ideas or plans?
- Are those who know the person concerned about a specific target or timeframe?
- Has the person previously come to someone's attention or raised concern in a way that suggested he or she needs intervention or supportive services?

It is important for the Team to ask of those who know the person in question whether they see the person as capable of violence. As people are often reluctant to see violence as a possibility, if the Team learns that someone in the person's life does think the person is capable of violence, this should raise the Team's concern considerably. However, the Team should recognize that some people — such as parents, significant others, or anyone else who is very close with the person in question — may not see the potential for violence even if others do. Those in close relationships with a person may be too close to the person/situation to admit violence is possible or even likely.

### k.   *What circumstances might affect the likelihood of violence?*

- What factors in the person's life and/or environment might increase or decrease the likelihood that the person will engage in violent behavior?
- What is the response of others who know about the person's ideas or plans? (Do they actively discourage the person from acting violently, encourage the subject to attack, deny the possibility of violence, passively collude with an attack, etc.?)

This question underscores the principle that violence risk is dynamic. All of us are capable of violence under the right (or wrong) circumstances. By asking this question, the Team can identify what factors in the person's life might change in the near- to mid-term, and whether those changes could make things better or worse for the person in question. If things look like they might improve for the person, the Team could monitor the person and situation for a while and re-assess after some time has passed. If things look like they might deteriorate, the Team can develop a management plan (if they believe the person poses a threat of harm or self-harm) or a referral plan (if the person does not pose a threat but appears in need of help) to help counteract the downturn in the person's circumstances. The Team may also be able to take steps to change the negative situation. One role that a team can play is to change systemic problems where they exist. The person may have acted inappropriately, but may have done so in response to a legitimate grievance or systemic problem. The Team can serve as a catalyst to change those systemic conditions for the better.

### l.   *Where does the subject exist along the pathway to violence?*
(See Figure 1 in Section Two)

- Has the subject:
  - o   developed an idea to do harm?
  - o   developed a plan?
  - o   taken any steps toward implementing the plan?
  - o   developed the capacity or means to carry out the plan?
- How fast is he/she moving toward engaging in harm?

- Where can the Team intervene to move the person off that pathway toward harm?

---

### Using Instruments to Assist the Assessment Process

There are various instruments the TAM Team can use to assist in this assessment process. These objective tools can be very helpful when used appropriately. We caution, however, that the TAM Team should not rely too heavily on the use of these instruments. The assessment process should always be guided primarily by human judgment.

**Utilize appropriate, objective, instruments, e.g.:**
- Cawood / White Assessment Grid;
- Classification of Violence Risk (COVR);
- MOSAIC;
- Spousal Assault Risk Assessment Guide (SARA);
- Violence Risk Appraisal Guide (VRAG);
- Workplace Assessment of Violence Risk (WAVR-21);
- Workplace Violence Risk Assessment Checklist.

*Note*: This is a partial listing of such instruments and not an endorsement of any particular approach.

**Appropriate use of instruments:**[66]
- Utilize instruments that are designed for the population of concern;
- Avoid reliance on instrument only;
- Ensure evaluator is properly trained;
- Ensure that instrument is reliable and valid;
- Be aware of limitations of the instrument;
- Stay current with new data and versions;
- Integrate information with structured professional judgment.

---

### 5.  Make the assessment.

Once the Team has answered the above questions (recognizing that a team may not be able to obtain information regarding all of the

---

66  Association of Threat Assessment Professionals (2006). *Risk assessment guideline elements for violence: Considerations for assessing the risk of future violent behavior.* Los Angeles: Authors.

questions) and documented its answers, it then assesses the threat posed by the individual by answering the following two ultimate assessment questions:

**A.   *Does the person pose a threat of harm, whether to him/herself, to others, or both? That is, does the person's behavior suggest that he or she is on a pathway toward harm?*[67]**

If the answer is "no," the Team documents its response and reasoning and proceeds to Question B.

If the answer is "yes," the Team documents its response and rationale, and then proceeds to develop, implement, and continually monitor an individualized threat management plan to reduce the risk that the person poses (see Step 6). The Team should document the details of this plan, as well as document steps it takes to implement the plan and/or refer the person for help. The Team should also document its efforts to monitor the effectiveness of the plan and modify the plan as needed. The Team does not need to answer Question B, which pertains to assistance provision for persons who do not pose a threat, as any needs for assistance and intervention for persons who do pose a threat will be addressed in the threat management plan.

**B.   *If the person does not pose a threat of harm, does the person otherwise show a need for help or intervention, such as mental health care?***

If the answer is "no," the Team documents its response, records the person and incident in the Team's incident database, and closes the inquiry. There is no need to proceed to Steps 6, 7 or 8.

If the answer is "yes," the Team documents its response and rationale, and then develops, implements, and re-evaluates a plan to monitor the person and situation and/or connect the person with resources in order to assist him/her with solving problems or addressing needs. The Team should document the details of this plan, as well as document steps taken to implement the plan and/or refer the person for help. The Team should also document its efforts to monitor the effectiveness of the plan and modify the plan as needed. We recommend the Team review the options listed in Step 6 in crafting its monitoring and referral plan.

The answers to Questions A and B will dictate the Priority Level that the TAM Team assigns to the case. The Priority Level is designed to communicate both the level of threat posed by the person in question, as well as actions that may be necessary on the part of the Team to address

---

67   Fein et al., 2002.

and reduce that threat level. While the Team can choose its own rating scale, we offer the following for consideration.

## Table 4: Sample Priority Levels for Threat Cases

**Priority 1 (Extreme Risk)**
The person/situation appears to pose a clear and immediate threat of serious violence toward self or others and requires containment. The Team should immediately notify law enforcement to pursue containment options, and/or take actions to protect identified target(s). Once such emergency actions have been taken, the Team shall then develop and implement a management plan in anticipation of the person's release or return to campus.

**Priority 2 (High Risk)**
The person/situation appears to pose a threat of self-harm or physical violence, usually to an identifiable target, but currently lacks immediacy and/or a specific plan — or a specified plan of violence does exist but currently lacks a specific target. This requires the Team to develop and implement a management plan.

**Priority 3 (Moderate Risk)**
The person/situation does not appear to pose a threat of violence or self-harm at this time, but does exhibit behaviors/circumstances that are likely to be disruptive to the community. This case warrants some intervention, referral and monitoring to minimize risk for significant disruption to the community or escalation in threat. The Team should develop a referral and/or active monitoring plan.

**Priority 4 (Low Risk)**
The person/situation does not appear to pose a threat of violence or self-harm at this time, nor is their evidence of significant disruption to the community. This case may warrant some intervention, referral and monitoring to minimize risk for escalation in threat. The Team should develop a monitoring plan.

**Priority 5 (No Identified Risk)**
The person/situation does not appear to pose a threat of violence or self-harm at this time, nor is their evidence of significant disruption to the community. The Team can close the case without a management or monitoring plan, following appropriate documentation.

*Source: Deisinger & Randazzo (2008)*

---

_Decision Point_: **How will your team handle assistance cases?**

Some colleges and universities do not have designated student assistance teams or programs in place, and even fewer have separate teams for handling the assistance of faculty and staff. In some cases, these teams are combined. In these situations, the institution must decide how it would like to handle those cases in which a threat is not posed but assistance is required. We recommend that pre-existing teams and programs be utilized for this purpose, rather than creating new ones. There is no single model or gold standard here. It is important, however, that every institution has in place a process for screening cases, and that some mechanism is identified for ensuring that the case is managed by the appropriate authorities for either threat assessment or assistance provision.

---

6.  **Develop and implement a plan to manage and/or monitor the person.**[68]

If the Team determines that the person in question poses a threat of violence or suicide, it then needs to develop, implement, and monitor an individualized plan to intervene and reduce that threat. The plan should be based upon the information gathered in the threat assessment inquiry, and tailored to address the problems of the person in question. Threat management is more art than science. It focuses both on addressing what is already working for the person of concern, and creatively searching for resources — both on- and off-campus — that are available to help move the person away from thoughts and plans of violence/suicide and get assistance to address underlying problems.

The following are options the Team can consider in crafting an individualized threat management plan. These should not be considered exhaustive of all available options; individual institutions may identify other options available in addition to — or in place of — the following:

- **Engage with the person** - An engagement model works well with the majority of cases. Most persons who come to the attention of TAM Teams are persons who are at a crisis point and are looking for assistance. Most have distanced themselves from others or feel alienated from others. They typically respond positively to someone who will hear their concerns, who will not over-react to emotional venting, who will engage in problem-solving, and who demonstrates care for them and their situation.

---

68  Calhoun & Weston, 2003; Fein et al., 2002; Mohandie, 2000.

While this model often works well, there are some cases in which such direct engagement might inflame the situation. Therefore, each situation should be evaluated based on its own case facts in order to determine whether such direct follow-up would be appropriate.

- **Monitor the situation** - Sometimes, the best initial approach is to "wait and see." Clearly, this approach should only be taken when there are no indications of imminent or high risk. The Team may decide to keep an eye on the person and their situation to see how things may evolve over a few days, weeks, or months. In some cases, the Team may decide to monitor a person as the only step it takes. In others, the Team may use monitoring as one part of an overall plan. Monitoring can take more passive or more active forms. In more active monitoring, the Team may solicit the help of those who know the person and see him or her on a regular basis. This can include roommates, friends, family members, significant others, etc., whom the Team asks to keep an eye on the person and alert the Team if there is any change in behavior or other concerns. Active monitoring involves the Team checking the status of the situation on a proactive basis, until the situation is adequately resolved. Passive monitoring involves asking reporting parties to keep the team informed if there are any significant developments in the case. The Team will not actively check the status of the situation unless additional information lead them to do so. For passive monitoring to be most effective, persons who raised initial concerns may need to be trained and coached in regard to indications of problematic changes in the system. If the person(s) expressing concern have not received basic awareness training, this would be a good time to build that relationship and provide such training.

- **Identify an ally or trusted person** - A key to establishing an effective working relationship with the person of concern is to identify a responsible person they already trust. One key step to defusing a potentially violent situation involving someone with a grievance is to allow him or her to feel "heard" and validated. Even if they cannot get their way — which oftentimes they cannot — feeling as if someone has understood their position can go a long way toward moving the person away from thoughts and plans of violence. The trusted ally can be a friend, fellow student, colleague, faculty advisor, mentor, coach, supervisor, residential advisor, spouse, or parent. If the Team cannot find someone that the person already trusts, they can use someone in the campus community who relates well with most people.

- **Family / Parental notification** - Depending on the circumstances of the case, the Team may decide that it would be beneficial to notify the person's family or parents. The Team should first assess whether doing so could exacerbate or harm the current situation, or otherwise make things worse for the person in question. If the Team determines it would not, then it may opt to contact the person's family (e.g., spouse, significant other, parents, etc.). To make this determination, the Team should obtain sufficient information from the person in question or from others who know him/her, to help determine whether family members will be effective allies and supports. It must be understood that not all spouses, significant others, or parents have the skills or abilities to provide assist to a relative or spouse in need, and that some will actively make situations worse through their involvement.

- **Law enforcement intervention** - In some situations, it may be necessary for the TAM Team to involve campus law enforcement and/or local law enforcement to help handle the person and/or situation. The Team should first consider whether law enforcement intervention will exacerbate the situation unnecessarily.

- **Behavioral contract** - This is an agreement that is established between an institutional representative and the person of concern. The purpose is to get the person to agree to engage in certain behaviors (e.g., attend class regularly or complete work assignments in a timely manner), agree to stop performing certain behaviors (e.g., classroom disruptions), or both — in exchange for something the person wants, such as a chance to continue enrollment or maintain a position. Behavioral contracts set forth clear guidance of what is expected of the person, what they will get in return for complying with those parameters, and what natural consequences they face if they fail to do so. Some behavioral contracts also include a type of "amnesty clause" or "escape clause" that provides the person an option — usually an ally to seek out for assistance — if they find themselves in a situation where they believe or fear they will not be able to adhere to the contract. This option can be used in cases in which there may be times or situations where adherence is more difficult, and provides another layer of support in those situations to help the person continue to succeed.

- **Mandated psychological assessment or hospitalization** - The team leader or some other member of the Team should maintain a liaison with the mental health professional performing the psychological assessment of the person in question and coordinate the person's return to the institution if possible.

Team members should be knowledgeable about relevant state laws and procedures regarding involuntary evaluation or hospitalization. Typically, such laws require that the person demonstrate at least one of the following *as a result of an apparent mental illness*:

o Being an imminent danger of serious injury or death to self;

o Being an imminent danger of serious injury or death to others;

o Being grossly incapable of providing for basic survival needs (shelter, safety, food, medication, etc.).

State laws will provide guidance as to procedures for civil commitment for evaluation and/or treatment, including who has the authority to request them, as well as emergency committal for such services. A team might move to hospitalize a student, faculty or staff member who shows the elements listed above.

When team members facilitate or become aware of such committals, they should work with the person of concern and the mental health professionals to share information and to obtain the appropriate releases to facilitate effective continuity of care.

Psychological assessment is appropriate when the person indicates that their behavior is a result of a psychological condition, or when their behavior might indicate (to a reasonable lay person) that such is the case. The primary purposes of such evaluations are to assess functioning and needs and to recommend relevant treatment or interventions.

Such assessments may be provided through on-campus mental health professionals or off-campus resources, but should be coordinated by an office or staff member outside of the campus health or counseling center. That office will not be bound by confidentiality in the same way as health service providers and can keep the Team informed about the status of the case, while being respectful of the individual's privacy regarding details of the evaluation.

There is another level of assessment that might also be appropriate when a student, faculty or staff member has demonstrated a pattern of severe or chronic behavior that calls into question their ability to function safely and/or effectively as a student or as a professional. These evaluations in the workplace are often referred to as fitness-for-duty evaluations. Such evaluations should be used with care to be sure that they are appropriate for the situation. They should always be conducted by an independent examiner who is NOT involved in the person's treatment. The examiner should be properly licensed and qualified to conduct such evaluations. While the examiner should be retained by the institution in order to address its concerns, it is often best if the examiner is not an employee of the institution, so as to minimize real and perceived conflicts of interest. The institution should make clear to the examiner the relevant question(s) to be addressed. The focus of the examination will differ depending upon whether the goal of the assessment is to determine if the person is stable enough to pursue their academic/professional goals or to determine whether the person poses an ongoing threat of violence. A thorough examination would be one that assesses the subject's ability to safely AND effectively perform the essential duties of their position. Note the emphasis on safely AND effectively! Institutions should review the examiner's background, training and experience in addressing BOTH types of questions.

- **Options for leave or separation from the institution** - The TAM Team may have several options for temporary or permanent separation of the person of concern from the institution. These include the following:

    o **Voluntary leave** - The Team can request that the person in question voluntarily leave the campus for a period of time.

    o **Interim suspension** - The Team can request that the college or university suspend the person in question from his/her roles as a student or employee for a period of time.

    o **Involuntary leave** - The Team can request that the college or university require the person in question to leave campus for a period of time.

    o **Removal from housing** - If the person in question is a student residing on campus, the Team can request that the college or university remove him or her from housing for a period of time.

With respect to leave, suspension, and termination options (and any options that focus solely on controlling the person of concern), it may be tempting for institutions to think that getting the student or staff person of concern off campus eliminates any threat posed. However, it is important to keep in mind that doing so does not solve the long-term problem of moving the person away from thoughts and plans of violence and getting them connected to resources that can help address underlying issues. More importantly, once the person of concern is no longer connected to the campus, it means the Team has far fewer — if any — eyes and ears available to monitor how the person is doing and to promote engagement with the person. While such measures are required in some situations, they should not be implemented in the absence of a full assessment of the person and implementation of other case management strategies to solve the longer-term problems that are prompting the difficult behavior in the first place.

- **Modification of the environment** - While there are many ways to consider intervention directly with the subject of concern, some situations will be best resolved by modifications to the system or environment that may be causing or contributing to the concern. For example, a student may react inappropriately to a poorly developed and burdensome procedure or policy. The student's behavior must be addressed, but if the procedure or policy tends to provoke discord because it is objectively unfair or unreasonable, then that procedure or policy may be reviewed and revised to be more useful and helpful.

- **Victim protective actions** - In addition to interventions with the subject (or in cases where it is not possible to intervene effectively with a subject or where the Team is dealing with an anonymous threat), emphasis may be placed on actions that increase the potential victim's safety regardless of the subject's actions. Such protective efforts may include:

  o Administrative leave for the potential victim to minimize exposure to the potential danger;

  o Moving the potential victim to another housing or work location so they are harder to locate or are in a more secure environment;

  o Modifying security and access control of the potential victim's housing or work area (e.g., locking access doors or verifying identity before providing access);

  o Coaching potential victims regarding personal safety approaches (e.g., monitoring and being aware of their environment, varying their routes of travel, traveling with friends/colleagues, etc.).

## 7.   Monitor the plan.[69]

Threat management cases generally remain open until the person in question is no longer reasonably assessed to pose a threat (as described in the steps above). This may be well beyond when criminal cases are closed or mental health services are completed. The Team should continue to monitor the plan, and modify it as needed, for as long as the individual might still pose a threat. A person can continue to pose a threat

---

69   Calhoun & Weston, 2003; Fein et al., 2002; Mohandie, 2000.

even after he/she ceases to be a member of the campus community. Take, for example, a case in which a threatening student graduates and then moves off-campus. It is still very easy for this person to come back to campus and cause harm. Therefore, the TAM Team should continue to monitor the situation through its relationship with local law enforcement agencies and mental health agencies, as well as in direct cooperation with the person where possible.

## 8. Refer and follow up as appropriate.

In many ways, threat cases are never truly closed. For a long period of time, it may be necessary for the Team to make further referrals for the individual and/or take other follow-up steps as needed. The TAM Team should be particularly aware of important and meaningful dates or events that may trigger a person to become a threat, such as anniversaries, failing a course, termination of benefits, the ending of relationship, or the occurrence of mass attacks elsewhere.

It is important for the TAM Team to understand that a person does not simply become a threat and then cease to be a threat. A person's risk level fluctuates over the course of his/her life, since life itself is a dynamic and ever-changing process. This is why it is so vitally important for the TAM Team to form strong relationships with other departments and institutions, both on- and off-campus, that can keep the Team informed and updated. Maintaining an open line of communication and brainstorming with others is what enables the TAM Team to effectively manage a person over the course of time.

Finally, as a case is coming to an end, it may be helpful for the Team to request feedback from the individual in question. By giving the person an opportunity to discuss the threat assessment and management process from his/her perspective, the Team can identify those aspects of the process that are working well and those that may need improvement. See Appendix D for a sample TAM Team feedback form.

In summary, Figure 3 provides a flow chart depiction of the threat assessment and management process as outlined in this section.

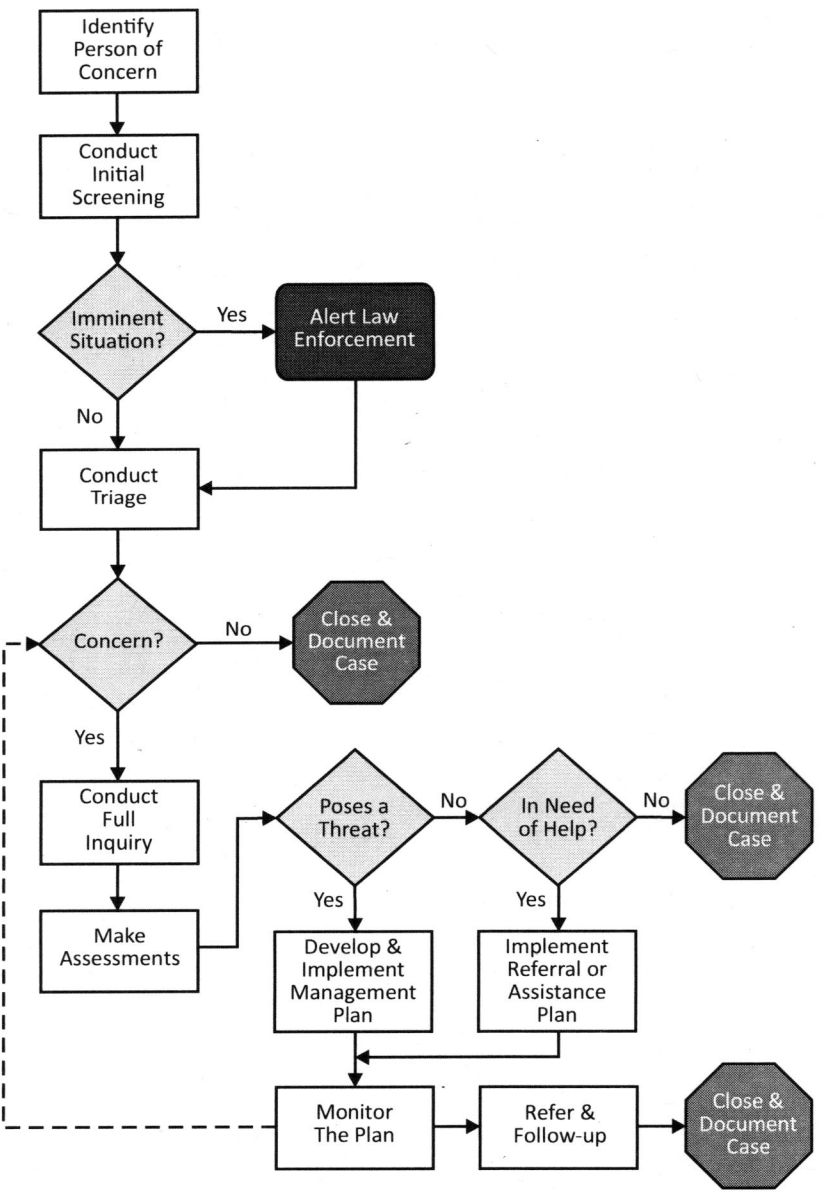

**Figure 3: Threat Assessment and Management Flow Chart**

# Section Five

## Team Operations and Communication

# Team Operations and Communication

Effective TAM Teams operate with a clear sense of mission and purpose, and with the full authority of the leadership of the institution. The authority for such a team should be clearly addressed through institutional policy and procedures and support of senior administration. The Team should be authorized to engage in activities that reduce the risk of threatening situations. In circumstances where team members (individually or collectively) do not have the authority to take particular actions (such as modifying institutional policy or procedures), the Team should have direct access to senior administrators who possess such authority.

---

### Starting a New TAM Team

When creating a TAM Team from scratch, the Team must operate with authority from the college or university's executive leadership. Then, an initial kick-off workshop should be held, at which the Team should develop its mission statement, guiding principles, and strategic plan. This workshop should be held immediately, so that these issues can be agreed upon and outlined as quickly as possible, as they will guide the Team's work from that point on. If needed, the Team can bring in an outside consultant or agency to assist in its initial start-up process. This is helpful to establish a mission, clarify goals, identify key team membership, outline team processes, and develop a plan to address barriers to implementation.

---

### Basic Operations

A team should meet with sufficient frequency and regularity to meet several goals including:

1. *Development of Effective Working Relationships between Team Members.*
   Team members must have a clear understanding of the resources, capabilities, limitations and interpersonal communication styles of other team members. The midst of a crisis is not an ideal time

to begin to work through these issues, which are so critical for the operation of any effective team.

2.  *Timely and Effective Management of Cases.*
    The threshold set for involvement of the TAM Team will be a key variable in determining the Team's caseload. The Team must decide upon the level of concern required to trigger the threat assessment process. Here, an optimal balance must be sought between the capabilities of the Team and a sufficiently low threshold of concern that allows for early identification and intervention with problematic situations. The lower the threshold, the higher the caseload will be — and therefore, the greater the frequency of communication and meetings to manage the cases.

---

*Decision Point*:  **What should be your team's threshold for information?**

Each TAM Team should define its threshold with regards to the level of behavior or concern that should trigger a notice to the Team. There is a tradeoff between early identification and managing the workload. A low threshold of concerning behavior will facilitate early identification and intervention, will allow for a broader range of management options, and may thereby reduce the likelihood of cases escalating to crisis levels. However, the more information the Team receives, the greater the Team's workload and the greater the risk of becoming overwhelmed.

Conversely, a high threshold of concern will reduce the overall workload but may result in the Team not becoming aware of situations until later in their development when there are likely to be greater crises and diminished range of appropriate options.

The optimal threshold will vary by the culture of the institution, the mission of the Team, the Team's capacity and resources, and relevant laws that may govern the operation of such a team.

---

3.  *Effective Follow-up.*
    Teams must engage not only in timely assessment and intervention with new cases, but also in timely and regular follow-up with existing cases to monitor the effectiveness of interventions and situational changes that may impact upon the safety of the situation.

A good way for team members to start working together to achieve the above goals is by collaborating on a strategic plan for the Team and its operations. Having a strategic plan in place will help the Team decide on its overall purpose and core activities and will help drive the Team's initial work. In addition to long-term goals, the plan should also include the Team composition, roles and responsibilities, methods of record keeping, and the Team's budget. This is a plan that is intended to be subject to periodic review and revision at least once per year.

---

*Decision Point*:  **How often should your team meet?**

How often a TAM Team should meet depends on several factors, including the volume of cases handled, the capacity of the Team, and the degree to which Team members have other opportunities to work collaboratively with each other. Initially, regular and frequent Team meetings are recommended, with a primary focus on team members becoming knowledgeable about the roles of each team member and gaining experience in working with differing communication styles and problem-solving approaches. As the Team gains experience and confidence in working together, it may meet less frequently as dictated by case load and priority.

---

### Regular Duties and Responsibilities

While the frequency of meetings depends upon the factors mentioned above, we will provide some rough guidelines that we think might be helpful. The TAM Team has various duties and responsibilities, and the frequency with which particular tasks should be carried out range from once a day to once a year.

#### Daily Activities

The team leader or another designated person on the Team should screen for new cases on a daily basis. If a case seems in need of immediate attention, as in cases where there appears to be a threat of physical injury posed to the community or to an individual, the team leader (or any other member of the Team) can call for an emergency meeting of the entire group.

#### Weekly/Bi-weekly Activities

In addition to discussing new cases, the TAM Team also needs to review existing cases, follow up on previously assigned tasks, report on completion of previously discussed tasks, discuss management strategies, decide whether management of a particular case requires a broader level of representation, set the next action steps, assign responsibility for completion of action steps, set timelines for when those steps should be carried out, and determine how their success will be evaluated.

The frequency of meetings for reviewing new and old cases is dependent upon the Team's workload and experience in working together. Particularly when a TAM Team is newly formed, it should meet at least once every other week in order for the team members to become acquainted with each other and the threat assessment and management process, as well as to discuss other aspects of an effective threat assessment system where the Team could take the lead, such as in coordinating awareness training for the entire campus (see Section Seven for a full discussion on the components of an effective campus threat assessment capacity).

TAM Team meetings to review new and on-going cases should have a very organized structure and flow, which should be under the leadership of the team leader. Cases should always be discussed in order according to their priority level (see Table 4 in Section Four).

For each new case, the following issues should be addressed:
- Understand threats / concerns
- Identify immediately available information
- Determine imminence of situation
- Identify target (if not already known)
- Begin threat assessment process (see Section Four for details)
- Assign responsibilities and deadlines
- Document initial information

For on-going cases, the above issues should continue to be addressed, as well as the following:
- Continue guiding implementation of previously established strategies
- Re-evaluate threats
- Evaluate needs of community

Before the end of each TAM Team meeting, responsibility should be assigned to specific team members for implementing the recommendations that the Team has developed.[70] This helps to avoid confusion, ensuring that efforts are neither duplicated nor neglected. One person on the Team should be designated for monitoring team members' individual assignments to make sure that everyone does their part.[71]

## Monthly

About once per month, it would be beneficial for the TAM Team to measure its performance to determine if cases are being identified, assessed and managed effectively. The Team's work should be reviewed and compared to its strategic plan to determine whether the plan is being carried out successfully. If it is not, changes should be made accordingly. In addition, some form of outreach to the campus community should be conducted as frequently as once per month in order to encourage reporting. As discussed in Section Four, outreach to the campus community is a key factor in the TAM Team's ability to identify persons at risk. Because of the high turnover of students, faculty and staff at institutions of higher education, the TAM Team must conduct outreach efforts on a frequent and regular basis, encouraging members of the campus community to report suspicious or troubling behaviors and informing them about how this information can be reported.

## Semi-Annually

About twice per year, the TAM Team members should train together and conduct tabletop exercises or review cases for lessons learned. These trainings and exercises help to ensure that the Team is up-to-date on current threat assessment and management issues, and improves the team members' working relationships with each other. After-action reviews should be conducted in order to capture the lessons learned and update the Team's strategic plan. If needed, outside consultants, agencies, and/or institutions can be brought in for assistance.

## Annually

On a yearly basis, the TAM Team should meet to conduct strategic planning. The Team should take a long-term look at what needs to be done on campus in the upcoming year, such as faculty/staff training, outreach, tabletop exercises, and after-action reviews, and make

---

70  United States Postal Service Threat Assessment Team Task Force (1997). *Threat assessment team guide*. Washington, DC: U.S. Postal Service

71  United States Postal Service Threat Assessment Team Task Force, 1997.

plans accordingly. The Team's strategy should be clearly outlined, including the Team's mission, guiding principles, and members. The Team must carefully consider what has been working up until that point and what has not. Based upon knowledge and experience gained throughout the year and evaluation of the Team's case management and outreach, the Team's strategy should be amended as necessary. In addition, the TAM Team should continually strive to identify gaps in services provided to the campus community, and work collaboratively with on- and off-campus agencies to find ways to fill them.

# SECTION SIX

## INFORMATION SHARING AND RECORD KEEPING

# INFORMATION SHARING AND RECORD KEEPING

Two key components of the threat assessment and management process are (1) information sharing between the Team and those on- and off-campus who have information about a person of concern; and (2) keeping accurate and detailed records for each individual case.

## *Information Sharing Strategies and Legal Considerations*
A TAM Team can only be effective in its mission if it can access and share information about a person and/or situation that has raised some concern. As discussed in Section Three, it is important that the Team include legal counsel either on the Team or as an accessible resource for the Team. One of the key functions of this individual is to ensure that the Team adheres to laws protecting individuals' privacy and confidentiality, particularly the Health Insurance Portability and Accountability Act (HIPAA), the Family Educational Rights and Privacy Act (FERPA), and state and federal disability laws.[72] Through consultation with the institution's legal counsel, the TAM Team should become familiar with ways in which the Team can access and share information in order to best assess, respond to, and manage an array of threatening and concerning behavior on campus.

Before any further discussion, we want to emphasize that we are not attorneys and underscore that the following information should not be construed as legal advice. We strongly recommend that TAM Teams consult with their institution's legal counsel on these issues as they begin operations and as they encounter specific legal questions in individual cases.

That said, in our experience we have been able to share information within the parameters established by these laws and regulations. For the most part, these laws should not be an impediment to the TAM Team carrying out its duties. We offer the following suggestions for TAM Teams to consider, in consultation with their legal counsel:[73]

---

72  Dunkle, J. H., Silverstein, Z. B., & Warner, S. L. (2008). Managing violent and other troubling students: The role of threat assessment teams on campus. *Journal of College and University Law, 34*(3), 585-636.

73  For an overview of the laws and regulations that impact threat assessment teams, please see Dunkle et al. (2008).

FERPA:

- FERPA protects the privacy of information in a student's educational records. It is designed to prohibit the inappropriate disclosure of student educational information beyond those who have a legitimate educational need to know. However, institutions can and should identify TAM Team members in their FERPA policies as among those educational officials with a legitimate need to know information in educational records.

- FERPA provisions also include exceptions that allow information sharing in the case of emergency situations and/or situations where public safety is a concern. Guidance issued by the U.S. Department of Education[74] (which enforces FERPA) following the Virginia Tech shooting has made clear that it is up to individual institutions to decide whether there is an emergency or public safety concern. As long as the TAM Team documents why it felt there was an emergency and/or threat to public safety, there should be no concerns about sharing information.

- FERPA pertains only to the privacy of records; it does not extend to communications, observations, and other forms of information that team members may need to share. This means that team members are free to ask — and faculty and staff are free to share — their observations about a student, verbal communications with that student, and anything else not written down.

- FERPA does not pertain to law enforcement unit records. For this reason, institutions may wish to establish their TAM Team under the umbrella of the institution's police department, designated law enforcement entity, or unsworn security operation.

- Finally, FERPA does not permit a private right of action, meaning that individuals or institutions cannot be held liable for violations of FERPA. The law provides that federal funding could be withheld or fines could be assessed in cases where a pattern or practice of violations is present (as opposed to isolated violations, which are not individually sanctionable). To date, there have been no instances where an institution has received monetary sanctions for violating FERPA. Rather, it is more likely that an institution would receive some additional training from the U.S. Department of Education if it were found to have shared information in violation of FERPA.

---

74 U.S. Department of Education (October 2007). *Balancing student privacy rights and school safety: A guide to the* Family Educational Rights and Privacy Act *for Colleges and Universities*. Washington, DC: U.S. Department of Education. Available at *http://www.ed.gov/policy/gen/guid/fpco/brochures/postsec.html*, retrieved October 29, 2008.

HIPAA:

- HIPAA protects the confidentiality of information in health and mental health records. In addition, state laws also protect the confidentiality of mental health information and discussions between a patient and a mental health professional.

- HIPAA may not govern health and mental health records at university counseling centers (FERPA may apply instead). An institution's legal counsel should be consulted as to which regulations apply.

- HIPAA and state laws include exceptions where information can be shared in situations where a patient is a threat to themselves or others. In such situations where a mental health professional is aware that his/her patient has threatened harm to themselves or to someone else, the mental health professional has the duty to warn someone or to do something to protect the victim in question.[75]

- While HIPAA and state laws may prevent a mental health professional from disclosing information to the TAM Team, it does not prohibit mental health professionals from _receiving_ information about a patient. The TAM Team can provide the information it knows to an individual's therapist or counselor. In many cases, a treating mental health professional may only have partial information about a patient/client. Receiving information from the TAM Team about a particular individual may enhance the treatment that the mental health professional is able to provide.

- If the Team provides information to a mental health professional, it can then ask the mental health professional whether the new information received from the Team elevates their concern about the patient to the point where they now have a duty to warn or a duty to protect. If the information raises concern to that level, the mental health professional may be able to share information with the Team.

- Under HIPAA and state laws, confidentiality is held by the client or patient, not the mental health professional. Therefore, the TAM Team can always ask the person in question for their permission to access their mental health records and talk with their mental health professional. If approached with sincerity for their well-being and

---

75  States vary as to whether they impose a duty to warn or a duty to protect on mental health professionals in that state. We recommend that TAM team members become familiar with requirements in their state, so that they can interact more knowledgably with mental health professionals in specific cases and for liaison activities with local mental health professionals in general.

assurance that the Team can best help the person in question with full information and full access to everyone who may be in a position to help, it is quite likely that the person will consent. The Team will need to get the person's permission in writing.

- Finally, access to mental health information can be helpful in threat assessment cases, but it may not provide more detail than the Team is able to access through others who know or have observed the person in question. It is more important to consider incorporating any treating mental health professional into an individual case management plan.

Counseling and medical staff tend to be (appropriately) conservative and cautious in sharing information that, even if there are no legal or ethical prohibitions, would suggest any impropriety. For counseling and health services to be utilized and successful, patients must trust that the relationship is confidential and that such trust is inviolate, with the few legal exceptions that are standard in all states. However, according to both HIPAA and FERPA and many state patient privacy laws (check with your counsel on this), confidentiality only attaches when there is a working relationship with a specified client/patient. Therefore, if counseling or medical staff had information about a student, and that information was not from a confidential source (i.e., from another patient), they could share that information with others. From a practical standpoint, there would likely be few circumstances where counseling or medical staff would have such information. However, it is possible that they might observe or hear of situations outside of their professional roles. In that case, they would be legally free to share the information.

### Record Keeping
As the recipient and screener of all potentially threat-related information, it is helpful for the TAM Team to maintain a centralized database of everyone who has come to the Team's attention. It need not be complicated; a simple spreadsheet (one that can be searched for names, terms, etc.) would suffice. However, given the amount of information and the importance of accessing it easily and quickly, we do recommend that a database be used. This database can be used to store all information gathered throughout the threat assessment and management process. Or, the database can be used as more of an incident-tracking system that holds the names and other identifiers of everyone who is reported to the TAM Team. This system would enable the Team to cross-references the case file that contains the information relevant to that person and incident. Either way, even if a report does not seem to be a legitimate

threat now or the case is closed quickly, the individual's name should still
be noted in the database. If, at a later time, the individual's name comes
up again, the TAM Team will find information from this earlier report in
the database after "pinging" the system — that is, searching the database
for the name in question — and therefore be more informed about the
individual's pattern of behavior. Thus, this database provides a simple and
organized way to store, search, and retrieve information so that the TAM
Team can quickly know if a certain individual has come across the radar
screen previously.

---

_Decision Point_: **How should your team record and
maintain information?**

There are many ways the TAM Team can record and maintain
information; each college and university's TAM Team must select the
method that best suits its needs. "Depending on workload, managing
the information may require something as simple as an index card
system or as sophisticated as a computer database."[76]

---

By maintaining records and preserving evidence throughout the threat
assessment and management process, the TAM Team establishes a
legal and behavioral justification for intervention in order to reduce a
potential threat. Records that should be maintained by the Team include:
documentation of the individual's exact words and actions, including date,
time, behaviors, and witnesses; documentation of personal reactions and
protective actions taken by the individual; and copies of emails, memos,
voicemails, and other communications pertaining to the case. In addition,
the minutes of each TAM Team meeting should be carefully documented
and maintained.[77] All of these records should be stored in a secure,
centralized location 24 hours a day, 7 days a week.

The TAM Team's job is not done once a threat management plan has been
implemented. Rather, the Team must continue to monitor the individual
and the effectiveness of the steps that have been taken, continuing to
collect new evidence and continually re-assessing the situation over time.
Any additional discussions or information gathered regarding monitoring
and/or changes to a management plan should be documented as well.

---

76   Calhoun & Weston, June 2006, p. 3
77   Calhoun & Weston, June 2006, p. 3

## *Where to Store the Records?*

TAM Teams should consult with their respective counsel for guidance on this issue to be sure they are operating in accordance with federal and state laws, as well as institutional policies and procedures.

Some TAM Teams house their core records within their campus law enforcement or security operation. Such operations are typically staffed 24/7, facilitating access to case information when needed. This may facilitate an extra level of protection for such records — at least, those involving students. Law Enforcement Unit records "created and maintained by these law enforcement units are not considered education records subject to *FERPA*."[78] This may decrease undesirable access to such records (e.g., by the student under investigation) where such protection is seen as critical to maintaining the safety of the situation.

TAM Team members should establish clear and consistent understanding of expectations regarding documentation of their assessment, intervention, management and follow-up with cases that present for review. Teams should strive for a balance of record keeping that minimizes duplication of records (and efforts for the creation of those records) while maintaining sufficient documentation to facilitate case work, and that at the same time demonstrates compliance with law, policy and procedure.

---

78   U.S. Department of Education, October 2007, p. 2.

# SECTION SEVEN

## ADDITIONAL INSTITUTION COMPONENTS

# ADDITIONAL INSTITUTION COMPONENTS

In addition to establishing and maintaining a multidisciplinary TAM Team, there are several components that an institution can add to support and complement the Team's mission and overall effectiveness. These components include the following:

### Policies

In order to function, a TAM Team must have authority to receive reports; investigate and evaluate persons and situations that have raised concern; develop, implement, and monitor individual management plans; and record information about reports, incidents, investigations, assessments, and management plans. Therefore, it is important that an institution establish clear policies that enable the TAM Team to engage in such activities on behalf of the institution. These policies need not be overly complicated or detailed, but should be clear.

In order to further protect individuals who make such reports, the college or university should also have policies and procedures in place that strictly punish any acts of retaliation (see Appendix D for sample policies and procedures). Also, in order to discourage abuse of this communication system, the institution should also have a strict policy in place that punishes the intentional provision of false information to the Team.[79] All of the above policies and procedures should be made known to the entire campus community.

### Administration Support

If the Team does not already have clear support from key administrators on campus, they should work to achieve that support. A team can be more effective when they serve an institution whose leadership has made clear to the campus community that the Team is an important resource and that when the Team requests information or assistance, it is doing so on behalf of the administration. Some teams have found it helpful to bring in outside consultants to help formulate and secure this support.

---

79  Delaware Technical & Community College (2008). *Behavioral intervention and threat assessment* available at *http://www.dtcc.edu/stanton/safety/threat_assessment_policy.pdf*, retrieved August 21, 2008.

*Threat Assessment Training for the Team (Basic and Advanced)*
Prior to a team beginning its operations or shortly thereafter, we recommend that all members on the Team (or most, if all are not available) receive basic threat assessment training from qualified experts in the field of threat assessment. We also recommend that any new team members be given the same training when they join the Team. This can be accomplished through online/video training, attending conference presentations or workshops by recognized experts, receiving training from regional subject matter experts, or other comparable means. In addition, once the Team has completed basic training and has had the opportunity to work together for a while, we recommend that the Team receive advanced threat assessment training, including tabletop exercises at least once a year, preferably from a subject matter expert. Advanced training should allow the Team to walk through fictitious cases using their existing procedures, to have an opportunity to work together, and to identify where their procedures may need to be refined.

*Multiple Reporting Mechanisms*
The campus community should be able to report possible threats to the TAM Team 24 hours a day, 7 days a week. The more ways that students, faculty, staff, and parents can report concerns to the Team, the greater the likelihood that the Team will receive reports as early as possible. Many colleges and universities provide their community with a means of anonymous reporting, such as a single telephone number that can be used to provide information about a person in question without revealing information about the caller. While it may be helpful to have this means of anonymous reporting, we feel it is important that it not be the community's *only* means of communicating concerns about suspicious or troubling behavior. We recommend that the Team consider the various vehicles that can be used to facilitate reporting to the Team, including such low-tech options as periodic liaison discussions with each department to remind them that a student or colleague might come to them with some concerning information and that they can, in turn, report that information to the Team.

Rather than creating new ways to communicate information to the TAM Team, we recommend that each institution find ways to utilize mechanisms that already exist. For example, if the college or university already has a security webpage, then there is no need to create an entirely new one for reporting concerns to the TAM Team. Rather, a link to the Team can be provided through the pre-existing website. Similarly, if the institution already has an appropriate phone line in place, then it is better to use this phone number rather than create a new one for reporting concerns to the TAM Team. However, one should keep in mind that community members may not feel comfortable reporting a minor concern to the police; therefore, the phone number should connect the community with non-police personnel and be distinctly different from any emergency phone line used for reporting crimes. By using pre-existing mechanisms in this way, there is no need to introduce the campus community to something new. With no new phone number or website to memorize, it will be easier for the campus community to communicate their concerns to the Team.

### A Positive Emotional Climate

The Team's work can be enhanced through efforts to evaluate the overall emotional climate of the campus. A climate that is respectful and supportive of students, faculty, and staff is likely to have fewer threats and overall violence problems than a climate that tolerates or even encourages disrespect and unfair treatment.[80] The institution — or the Team — can assess the campus climate through surveys of students, faculty, staff, parents, alumni, and any others who have regular contact with the campus. The surveys can include, among other things, questions about how safe the respondents feel on campus, both physically and emotionally; questions that ask respondents to identify physical places and/or situations where they feel less safe or to rate a host of places and situations regarding how safe respondents feel in each one; and, questions regarding whether there is at least one person on campus that respondents feel they can turn to for assistance if needed. After conducting the survey and analyzing the results, it is important that the institution act on the findings to make any necessary enhancements. Involving students in the process of constructing the surveys and, even more importantly, in developing and implementing any improvements can in itself make students feel more connected to the campus.[81]

### A Proactive and Safety-Conscious Campus

A TAM Team can be particularly effective at an institution that already has a proactive approach to campus safety. We see threat assessment as an integral part of campus-wide efforts to prevent violence, identify persons at risk, intervene with developing concerns, respond to violent events, and recover from any violent events. We recommend that campuses consider conducting an overall vulnerability assessment, consistent with the International Association of Campus Law Enforcement Administrators

---

80  Fein et al., 2002.
81  Fein et al., 2002.

(IACLEA) *Blueprint for Safe Campuses,* and the Massachusetts Higher Education report, *Campus Violence Prevention and Response,* to identify areas where enhancement may be needed.[82]

### Campus-Wide Awareness Training

The Team can enhance reporting from throughout the campus if it advertises its existence and provides some guidance on the types of behaviors and concerns to report. One effective way to accomplish this is through periodic campus-wide awareness training, perhaps incorporated into existing events such as freshman orientation, residential advisor training, or convocation. Providing this training on a regular basis — or using other vehicles to remind the campus community periodically about the importance of reporting — can help address the challenge of campus turnover and maintain awareness about the Team. The overall message in campus awareness training should emphasize that the Team is dedicated to promoting campus safety and to helping persons who need assistance (rather than existing to punish or expel). Using a simple message such as that developed by the New York City Metropolitan Transportation Authority — "If you see something, say something"[83] — may be the easiest way for a team to promote its existence and encourage reporting.

### Consultation with Legal Counsel

Prior to starting its work, and periodically throughout the year, the TAM Team should consult with the institution's legal counsel regarding the laws and regulations that may impact its work. Legal counsel can also inform the Team of any new developments from case law or from changes in regulations (e.g., new guidance from the U.S. Department of Education regarding FERPA applications to threat assessment inquiries).

### Key Liaison Relationships

A TAM Team can enhance its effectiveness by developing and maintaining relationships with agencies and groups off campus that have some regular contact with parts of the campus community. Examples include local law enforcement, social services, community sports teams, volunteer programs, and popular local gathering spots. These agencies, organizations, and businesses may observe behavior that raises concern. If they know of the Team, they may be more inclined to notify the Team of their observations. Moreover, if they are aware of the Team and its

---

82  IACLEA, 2008; O'Neill et al., 2008.

83  State of New York Metropolitan Transportation Authority, *http://www.mta.info/mta/ security/index.html*

purpose, they may be more inclined to share information if the Team approaches them about a person of concern.

### Case Management Resources

Finally, the Team can best accomplish its ultimate goal of managing threatening situations by identifying in advance the range of resources that may be available on campus. These can include traditional resources such as counseling at the institution's mental health center; evaluation and treatment through a local mental health professional; and the involvement of law enforcement to contain or control the person in question. However, the Team should also consider less traditional options, such as a reduced course load, medical leave of absence, behavioral contracts, involvement in community service, assignment of a mentor, or any other resources that can help give the person in question something to look forward to or that plays to their strengths. Identifying a wide array of resources in advance will help the Team think broadly and creatively about options that may work when an individual case arises.

# CONCLUSION

# CONCLUSION

We believe that one of the most effective steps a college or university can take to improve the overall security and well-being of its community members is to establish a Threat Assessment and Management Team. This single step, which can help prevent not only targeted violence, but also various other problems such as suicide and alcohol/drug abuse, can be implemented immediately and at low cost. Most of the human resources are already available on campus or are readily accessible. In addition, unlike other security measures that colleges and universities might take to prevent violence (e.g., installation of surveillance cameras), establishing a TAM Team should generate little resistance or controversy. With the issuance of numerous reports on campus safety in the wake of the Virginia Tech and Northern Illinois shootings, there is widespread support for colleges and universities to establish TAM Teams. And as of this writing, two states now require their higher education institutions to have such teams.

However, as this Handbook has demonstrated, it is not enough to simply have a TAM Team in place; the Team is only worthwhile if it is run efficiently and effectively. This includes having a team leader who is highly inquisitive, devoted, and motivated to lead the Team, and having team members who are familiar with their specified roles and responsibilities. While a TAM Team can be established very quickly, it will take time for the team members to become acquainted with each other and with the threat assessment and management process. Members of a newly-formed TAM Team should attend trainings together, as this will help familiarize them with both the process and with each other's personal styles. In addition, it will take time for the TAM Team to establish working relationships with off-campus agencies such as mental health services and law enforcement. These relationships play a key role in identifying and managing threats quickly and effectively. It is also important that the TAM Team never lose sight of its long-term goals, which include continual outreach efforts to the community in order to encourage reporting and making sure the community is informed about the institution's anti-violence policies and procedures.

Finally, we want to stress that each college and university must design its TAM Team around the institution's specific needs, taking into account its unique situation, character, setting, population, and mission. Highlighted throughout this Handbook are "Decision Points" that each college or university must decide for itself, including how large the TAM Team should be, what its threshold of information should be, and how it should maintain its records. Because each institution is unique, the answers to these questions may vary widely. What matters most is that each institution consider these issues and decide on the most appropriate answer. There is no single right way to form and run a TAM Team. However, it is our hope that the guidance provided in this Handbook will help to make any team *effective*.

# BIBLIOGRAPHY

# BIBLIOGRAPHY

Association of Threat Assessment Professionals (2006). *Risk assessment guideline elements for violence: Considerations for assessing the risk of future violent behavior*. Los Angeles: Authors.

Borum, Fein, Vossekuil, & Berglund (1999). Threat assessment: Defining an approach for evaluating risk of targeted violence. *Behavioral Sciences & the Law, 17*, 323-337.

Braverman, M. (1999). *Preventing workplace violence: A guide for employers and practitioners*. London: Sage.

Calhoun, F. & Weston, S. (2003). *Contemporary threat management: A practical guide for identifying, assessing, and managing individuals of violent intent*. San Diego, CA. Specialized Training Services.

Calhoun, F. & Weston, S. (June 2006). Protecting judicial officials: Implementing an effective threat management process. *Bureau of Justice Assistance Bulletin, 1-8*. Washington, DC: U.S. Department of Justice, Office of Justice Programs, Bureau of Justice Assistance.

Corcoran, M.H. & Cawood, J.S. (2003). *Violence assessment and intervention: The practitioner's handbook*. New York: CRC.

DeBecker, G. (1997). *The gift of fear: And other survival signals that protect us from violence*. New York: Dell.

Delaware Technical & Community College (2008). *Behavioral intervention and threat assessment* available at *http://www.dtcc.edu/stanton/safety/ threat_assessment_policy.pdf*, retrieved August 21, 2008.

Delworth, U. (1989). Dealing with the behavioral and psychological problems of students. *New Directions for Student Services*, no. 45. San Francisco: Jossey-Bass.

Dunkle, J., Silverstein, Z. & Warner, S. (2008). Managing violent and other troubling students: The role of threat assessment on campus. *Journal of College and University Law, 34*(3), 585-636.

Fein, R. & Vossekuil, B. (1998). *Protective intelligence and threat assessment investigations: A guide for state and local law enforcement officials.* Washington, DC: U.S. Department of Justice, Office of Justice Programs, National Institute of Justice.

Fein, R., Vossekuil, B. & Holden, G. (September, 1995). Threat assessment: An approach to prevent targeted violence. *Research in Action, 1-7.* Washington, DC: U.S. Department of Justice, Office of Justice Programs, National Institute of Justice.

Fein, R., Vossekuil, B., Pollack, W., Borum, R., Modzeleski, W., & Reddy, M. (2002). *Threat assessment in schools: A guide to managing threatening situations and to creating safe school climates.* Washington, DC: U.S. Department of Education and U.S. Secret Service.

Flannery, R.B. (1995). *Violence in the workplace.* New York: Crossroad.

Gallagher, R. (2007). *National Survey of Counseling Center Directors 2007.* Alexandria, VA: International Association of Counseling Services, Inc.

Hoffman, A.M., Schuh, J.H., & Fenske, R.H. (Eds.). (1998). *Violence on campus: Defining the problems, Strategies for Action.* Gaithersburg, MD: Aspen.

International Association of Campus Law Enforcement Administrators (IACLEA). (1993). *Handling institutional violence on campus.* Hartford, CT: IACLEA.

IACLEA (1996). *Handling violence in the workplace.* Hartford, CT: IACLEA.

IACLEA (2008). *Overview of the Virginia Tech tragedy and implications for campus safety: The IACLEA Blueprint for safer campuses.* West Hartford, CT: IACLEA.

Jaeger, L., Deisinger, E., Houghton, D., & Cychosz, C. (1993). *A coordinated response to critical incidents.* Ames, IA: Iowa State University.

Lake, P. F. (June 2007). Higher education called to account: Colleges and the law after Virginia Tech. *Chronicle of Higher Education, 53*(43), B6.

Lazenby, R. (Ed.). (2007). *April 16: Virginia Tech Remembers.* New York: Plume.

Leavitt, M., Spellings, M., & Gonzalez, A. (2007). *Report to the President on issues raised by the Virginia Tech tragedy.* Washington, DC: U.S. Department of Health and Human Services, U.S. Department of Education, and U.S. Department of Justice.

Meloy, J.R. (2000). *Violence risk and threat assessment.* San Diego, Specialized Training Services.

Mohandie, K. (2000). *School violence threat management: A practical guide for educators, law enforcement, and mental health professionals.* San Diego, CA: Specialized Training Services.

Monahan, J. (1995). *The clinical prediction of violent behavior.* London: J. Aronson.

Monahan, J., Steadman, H.J., Silver, E., & Applebaum, P.S. (2001*). Rethinking risk assessment: The MacArthur study of mental disorder and violence.* New York: Oxford.

National Association of Attorneys General (2007). *NAAG task force on school and campus safety: Report and recommendations.* Washington, DC: National Association of Attorneys General.

O'Neill, D., Fox, J., Depue, R., Englander, E., et al. (2008). *Campus violence prevention and response: Best practices for Massachusetts Higher Education.* Boston, MA: Massachusetts Department of Higher Education.

Quinsey, V.L., Harris, G.T., Rice, M.E. & Cormier, C.A. (1998). *Violent offenders: Appraising and managing risk.* Washington, DC: American Psychological Association.

Randazzo, M., Borum, R., Vossekuil, B., Fein, R., Modzeleski, W., & Pollack, W. (2006). Threat assessment in schools: Empirical support and comparison with other approaches. In S.R. Jimerson and M.J. Furlong (Eds.), *The handbook of school violence and school safety: From research to practice.* Mahwah, NJ: Lawrence Erlbaum Associates, Inc.

Reddy, M., Borum, R., Vossekuil, B., Fein, R., Berglund, J., & Modzeleski, W., (2001). Evaluating risk for targeted violence in schools: Comparing risk assessment, threat assessment, and other approaches. *Psychology in the Schools, 38,* pp. 157-172.

Sluss, M. (2008, April 9). Governor signs Virginia Tech-inspired mental health reform bills. *The Roanoke Times*, http://www.roanoke.com/news/breaking/wb/157560, retrieved April 25, 2008.

State Journal-Register (2008, August 22). *Gov. signs bill requiring emergency plans at colleges.* Retrieved on October 22, 2008 from *http://www.sj-r.com/homepage/x633543415/Gov-signs-bill-requiring-emergency-plans-at-colleges.*

Suicide Prevention Resource Center (2004). *Promoting mental health and preventing suicide in college and university settings.* Newton, MA: Education Development Center, Inc.

The Jed Foundation (2008). *Student mental health and the law: A resource for institutions of higher education.* New York, NY: The Jed Foundation.

Turner, J. & Gelles, M. (2003), *Threat assessment: A risk management approach.* Binghamton, NY: Haworth Press.

United States Department of Education (October 2007). *Balancing student privacy rights and school safety: A guide to the* Family Educational Rights and Privacy Act *for colleges and universities.* Washington, DC: U.S. Department of Education.

United States Postal Service Threat Assessment Team Task Force (1997). *Threat assessment team guide.* Washington, DC: U.S. Postal Service

Virginia Tech Review Panel (2007). *Mass shootings at Virginia Tech, April 16, 2007: Report of the Review Panel presented to Governor Kaine, Commonwealth of Virginia.* Richmond, VA: Authors.

Vossekuil, B., Fein, R., Reddy, M., Borum, R., & Modzeleski, W. (2002). *The final report and findings of the Safe School Initiative: Implications for the prevention of school attacks in the United States.* Washington, DC: U.S. Department of Education and U.S. Secret Service.

# APPENDIX A

## DECISION POINTS

# APPENDIX A:  DECISION POINTS

_Decision Point_: **What should you call your team?**
Each college and university must decide what it would like to call its
threat assessment and management team. Many institutions may simply
prefer to call their team a "Threat Assessment Team." Others may be
concerned that incorporating the term "threat" may make the team
seem less approachable, less supportive, or may connote an adversarial
process, which goes against one of the guiding principles of threat
assessment and management. Therefore, another name may be chosen.
For example, we prefer the title "Threat Assessment and Management
Team" because it draws attention to the management function of the
team, which is extremely important and may be overlooked by focusing
solely on assessment. Other names that have been used include:

- Student Assistance Team
- Early Alert Team
- Behavioral Intervention Team
- Students of Concern
- Student Intervention Team
- Staff Intervention Team
- Campus Assistance Team
- Care Team

The team's name should reflect the values of the institution and the
mission of the team. For instance, if the team will only be focusing on
threats posed by students, then a name with "Student" in the title is
appropriate. Whatever its name, the team should go beyond the function
of a traditional student assistance team and incorporate the threat
assessment methodology discussed in this Handbook.

_Decision Point_: **How large should your team be?**
The size of the TAM Team will be determined, in large part, by the
team's workload and the resources of the institution.[84] For example, a
community college with several distinct campuses within a region may
opt either to have one large team with representatives from each campus
or smaller separate teams for each campus. Core team membership

---

84  Calhoun & Weston (June 2006).

should be driven by the communication and working relationships that are necessary to achieve the mission of the team. The institution can decide on the team's initial membership, and then expand or contract as conditions dictate. A general guide is to have as few core members as are necessary to provide for a timely and objective review of cases. Having more than five or six core members may make for difficult scheduling of regular meetings.

*Decision Point*: **How will your team handle assistance cases?**
Some colleges and universities do not have designated student assistance teams or programs in place, and even fewer have separate teams for handling the assistance of faculty and staff. In some cases, these teams are combined. In these situations, the institution must decide how it would like to handle those cases in which a threat is not posed but assistance is required. We recommend that pre-existing teams and programs be utilized for this purpose, rather than creating new ones. There is no single model or gold standard here. It is important, however, that every institution has in place a process for screening cases, and that some mechanism is identified for ensuring that the case is managed by the appropriate authorities for either threat assessment or assistance provision.

*Decision Point*:  **What should be your team's threshold for information?**
Each TAM Team should define its threshold with regards to the level of behavior or concern that should trigger a notice to the Team. There is a tradeoff between early identification and managing the workload. A low threshold of concerning behavior will facilitate early identification and intervention, will allow for a broader range of management options, and may thereby reduce the likelihood of cases escalating to crisis levels. However, the more information the Team receives, the greater the Team's workload and the greater the risk of becoming overwhelmed.

Conversely, a high threshold of concern will reduce the overall workload but may result in the Team not becoming aware of situations until later in their development when there are likely to be greater crises and diminished range of appropriate option.

The optimal threshold will vary by the culture of the institution, the mission of the Team, the Team's capacity and resources, and relevant laws that may govern the operation of such a team.

_Decision Point_:  **How often should your team meet?**
How often a TAM Team should meet depends on several factors, including the volume of cases handled, the capacity of the Team, and the degree to which Team members have other opportunities to work collaboratively with each other. Initially, regular and frequent Team meetings are recommended, with a primary focus on team members becoming knowledgeable about the roles of each team member and gaining experience in working with differing communication styles and problem-solving approaches. As the Team gains experience and confidence in working together, it may meet less frequently as dictated by case load and priority.

_Decision Point_: **How should your team record and maintain information?**
There are many ways the TAM Team can record and maintain information; each college and university's TAM Team must select the method that best suits its needs. "Depending on workload, managing the information may require something as simple as an index card system or as sophisticated as a computer database."[85]

---

85  Calhoun & Weston (June 2006)

# APPENDIX B

## CHECKLISTS

# APPENDIX B: CHECKLISTS

Here, we provide some checklists that we think will be helpful for colleges and universities in their efforts to establish and run an effective TAM Team. Please keep in mind that not every item we present will be applicable to your particular college or university's needs. You must determine what is best for your institution.

## SECTION ONE: DEFINITION AND PURPOSE

❑ Choose the name for your Threat Assessment and Management Team.

_____

## SECTION TWO: MISSION AND GUIDING PRINCIPLES

❑ Develop a written Mission Statement.

❑ Review the 12 guiding principles of threat assessment and management.

- ○ Targeted violence can be prevented
- ○ Violence is a dynamic process
- ○ Targeted violence is a function of several factors (target, individual, setting, triggering conditions)
- ○ Corroboration is critical
- ○ Threat assessment is about behavior, not profiles
- ○ Cooperating systems are critical resources
- ○ Does the person pose a threat?
- ○ Keep victims in mind
- ○ Early identification helps everyone
- ○ Multiple reporting mechanisms enhance early identification
- ○ Multi-faceted resources can provide effective interventions
- ○ Safety is a primary focus

## Section Three: Team Composition, Roles and Responsibilities

❑ Establish relationships with off-campus agencies that may prove helpful in the assessment and management process.

- ○ Local law enforcement
- ○ Mental health services
- ○ Others _____

❑ Identify the key members and size of your core team.

- ○ Consider the following factors:
  - ❑ Workload
  - ❑ The institution's resources

- ○ Ensure that the Team includes representatives from (or at least liaisons to) each of the following departments:
  - ❑ Academic Affairs / Provost
  - ❑ Human Resource Services (for cases involving faculty or staff members)
  - ❑ Media Relations
  - ❑ Police / Security
  - ❑ Residence Life (for colleges and universities with on-campus housing)
  - ❑ Student Affairs / Dean of Students (for cases involving students)
  - ❑ Mental Health Consultant
  - ❑ Legal Counsel
  - ❑ Graduate and Professional Schools
  - ❑ Specialty member (as determined on a case-by-case basis)

❑ Designate a team leader: _____

In choosing the team leader, consider the following desirable qualities:

- ○ Relates well with others
- ○ Has an inquisitive and skeptical mindset
- ○ Is familiar with threat assessment principles and practices
- ○ Has the appropriate resources upon which to draw

- ○ Has a good sense of judgment, objectivity, and thoroughness
- ○ Is passionate about the role and the work it entails

☐ Ensure that each team member is aware of his/her role and responsibilities.

☐ Gain access to outside experts or TAM Teams at other institutions that can be called upon in situations where expertise or assistance is needed.

☐ Train the members of your team together.

☐ Provide team members with opportunities to build working relationships with each other.

☐ Ensure that your team members _collectively_ possess the following skills and abilities:

- ○ Commitment to the safety of the campus community.
- ○ Commitment to fair, objective, reasonable and timely efforts to enhance the safety of the campus community.
- ○ Ability to recognize situations that may pose a concern to the safety, well-being, or effective operation of the campus community.
- ○ Ability to demonstrate sensitivity to a wide variety of issues and diversity of persons involved.
- ○ Ability to be flexible and open to creative problem-solving approaches.
- ○ Ability and willingness to share information through lawful and appropriate channels.
- ○ Ability to gather, organize, and interpret complex information, from multiple sources.
- ○ Ability to analyze problems and complaints by synthesizing information and observing behavior.
- ○ Knowledge of threat assessment, intervention, management, and communication techniques and procedures.
- ○ Ability to communicate effectively with difficult employees, students or others.
- ○ Ability to consult with employees and organizations to develop plans and strategies to alleviate problems.

○ Ability to document, prepare, update, and maintain confidential records.

○ Knowledge of college and university policies and procedures related to violence and campus safety.

○ Knowledge of state and federal laws related to privacy and confidentiality, including FERPA, HIPAA and Clery.

○ Knowledge of personnel and labor law issues, sufficient to advise management.

○ Ability to communicate and effectively present information (verbally and in writing) to a wide range of audiences, including senior administration, faculty, staff and students.

○ Ability to recognize the limits of their professional knowledge and skills.

○ Openness to seek out consultation when necessary.

○ Ability to work independently to complete designated responsibilities.

○ Ability to handle crisis communications.

○ Knowledge of community resources, such as social services and mental health professionals.

○ Ability to make critical decisions, assessments and recommendations.

○ Commitment to follow-up and resolution of situations

## SECTION FOUR: THE THREAT ASSESSMENT AND MANAGEMENT PROCESS

❑ Ensure that the team understands all the components of the Threat Assessment and Management process:

○ Identify a student, faculty member, or staff member who has engaged in threatening behaviors or done something that raised serious concern about their well-being, stability, or potential for violence or suicide.

○ Conduct an initial screening.

○ Conduct a full inquiry.

○ Answer key inquiry questions.

○ Make the assessment and define the priority of the case.

○  Develop and implement a plan to manage and/or monitor the person.

○  Monitor the plan.

○  Refer and follow up as needed.

○  Evaluate and seek feedback regarding the process and operation of the TAM Team.

❑  Conduct outreach and encourage the campus community to report troubling or suspicious behavior.

○  General awareness training about the TAM Team

○  Provide multiple ways for students, faculty, staff and others to report information

○  Provide periodic notification to parents

❑  Regularly "check in" with the following departments in order to identify students and employees who have raised some concern:

○  Student judicial process

○  Faculty grievance/conduct boards

○  Staff grievance review committees

○  Equal Opportunity & Diversity

○  University legal counsel

○  Campus police or security departments

○  Residential Life conduct boards

○  Honor boards

○  Greek Council and other student organizations

○  Local law enforcement

❑  Discuss with campus administrators, campus law enforcement, and/or local law enforcement what situations would constitute an "emergency" or "imminent situation."

❑  Maintain a database of *all* persons that come to the team's attention.

❑  For individual cases, the following steps constitute the threat assessment and management process:

○  Determine whether there is an emergency or imminent situation; if so, notify law enforcement immediately;

○ Gather information from various key sources to determine whether a full inquiry is necessary (assuming there is no imminent danger), including:
  ❑ Review of previous contacts made through threat assessment or assistance process ("pinging the system")
  ❑ Student affairs or human resources
  ❑ Campus police/security
  ❑ Academic affairs
  ❑ Residential staff
  ❑ Online searches

○ Ask the following triage questions to determine whether a fully inquiry is necessary:
  ❑ Has there been any mention of suicidal thoughts, plans, or attempts?
  ❑ Has there been any mention of thoughts/plans of violence?
  ❑ Have there been any behaviors that cause concern for violence or the person's well-being?
  ❑ Does the person have access to a weapon or are they trying to gain access?
  ❑ Are there behaviors that are significantly disruptive to the campus environment?

○ Consider the possible repercussions and consequences (i.e., potentially increasing the danger of the situation) before getting law enforcement involved when the person in question has broken the law.

○ If a full inquiry is necessary, gather additional information from various key sources:
  ❑ Faculty and staff members
  ❑ Student judicial process
  ❑ Faculty grievance/conduct boards
  ❑ Staff grievance review committees
  ❑ Equal Opportunity & Diversity
  ❑ University legal counsel
  ❑ Campus police or security departments
  ❑ Residential Life conduct boards
  ❑ Honor boards
  ❑ Greek Council and other student organizations

      ❑  Local law enforcement

      ❑  Previous schools / employers

      ❑  The person's family (if deemed appropriate)

      ❑  Email / Internet information

      ❑  Health / Counseling Center

◯ Consider using instruments to assist with the assessment process.

◯ Use information gathered to answer key inquiry questions:

      ❑  What are the person's motive(s) and goals?

      ❑  Have there been any communications suggesting ideas or intent to attack?

      ❑  Has the person shown inappropriate interest in any of the following?

           o  Workplace, school or campus attacks or attackers;

           o  Weapons (including recent acquisition of any relevant weapon);

           o  Incidents of mass violence (terrorism, workplace violence, mass murderers);

           o  Obsessive pursuit, stalking or monitoring others.

      ❑  Has the person engaged in attack-related behaviors (i.e., any behavior that moves an idea of harm forward toward actual harm)?

      ❑  Does the person have the capacity to carry out an act of targeted violence?

      ❑  Is the person experiencing hopelessness, desperation and/or despair?

      ❑  Does the person have a trusting relationship with at least one responsible person (e.g., a friend, significant other, roommate, colleague, faculty advisor, coach, parent, etc.)?

      ❑  Does the person see violence as the acceptable, desirable, or only way to solve problems?

      ❑  Is the person's conversation and "story" consistent with his or her actions?

      ❑  Are other people concerned about the person's potential for violence?

      ❑  What circumstances might affect the likelihood of violence?

      ❑  Where does the subject exist along the pathway to violence?

○ To make the assessment, answer the following questions:

  ❏ Does the person pose a threat of harm, whether to him/herself, to others, or both? That is, does the person's behavior suggest that he or she is on a pathway toward harm?

  ❏ If the person does not pose a threat of harm, does the person otherwise show a need for help or intervention, such as mental health care?

○ Consider all of the following options when designing an individualized threat management plan:

  ❏ Engage with the person

  ❏ Identify an ally or trusted person

  ❏ Family/parental notification

  ❏ Law enforcement intervention

  ❏ Behavioral contract

  ❏ Mandated psychological assessment or hospitalization

  ❏ Modification of the environment

  ❏ Victim protective actions

○ Continue to evaluate and modify the threat management plan for as long as the person in question is considered to be a threat.

## SECTION FIVE: TEAM OPERATIONS AND COMMUNICATION

❏ Ensure that your team operates with authority from the college or university's executive leadership.

❏ Develop a Strategic Plan.

❏ Determine how often your team should meet.

_____

Consider the following factors and goals:

○ How long your team has been in existence

○ The volume of cases

○ The team's threshold of information

❏ Ensure that your team meetings have an organized structure and flow.

❏ Ensure that the team discusses cases according to their priority level.

❑ On a daily basis:

  ○ Screen new cases.

❑ On a weekly/biweekly basis:

  ○ Review existing cases.

  ○ Follow up on previously assigned tasks.

  ○ Report on completion of previously discussed tasks.

  ○ Discuss management strategies.

  ○ Decide whether management of a particular case requires a broader level of representation.

  ○ Set the next action steps.

  ○ Assign responsibility for completion of action steps.

  ○ Set timelines for when those steps should be carried out.

  ○ Determine how success will be evaluated.

❑ On a monthly basis:

  ○ Measure team performance to determine if cases are being identified, assessed and managed effectively.

  ○ Review work and compare it to the team's strategic plan to determine whether the plan is being carried out successfully.

  ○ Conduct outreach to the campus community.

❑ On a semi-annual basis:

  ○ Train team members together and conduct tabletop exercises.

  ○ Conduct after-action reviews.

  ○ Update the team's strategic plan accordingly.

  ○ Bring in outside consultants, agencies, and/or institutions for assistance if needed.

❑ On a yearly basis:

  ○ Meet to conduct strategic planning.

  ○ Clearly outline the team's strategy, including the team's mission, guiding principles, and members.

  ○ Consider what has been working up until that point and what has not.

  ○ Amend the team's procedures as necessary.

- ○ Strive to identify gaps in services provided to the campus community.
- ○ Work collaboratively with on- and off-campus agencies to find ways to fill these gaps.

## SECTION SIX: INFORMATION SHARING AND RECORD KEEPING

- ❑ Ensure that your team understands privacy and confidentiality regulations, as well as relevant exceptions to each.
  - ○ HIPAA
  - ○ FERPA
  - ○ State confidentiality laws
  - ○ Ensure that your team adheres to disability laws.
    - ❑ State disability laws
    - ❑ Federal disability laws

- ❑ Become familiar with legal strategies for sharing information.

- ❑ Select what method your team should use for recording and maintaining information (e.g., index cards, computer database).

  _____

- ❑ Keep records of all pertinent information.
  - ○ Documentation of the individual's exact words and actions
    - ❑ Date
    - ❑ Time
    - ❑ Behaviors
    - ❑ Witnesses
  - ○ Documentation of personal reactions and protective actions taken by the individual
  - ○ Copies of all communications pertaining to the case
    - ❑ Emails
    - ❑ Memos
    - ❑ Voicemails

- ❑ Store all records stored in a secure, centralized location 24 hours a day, 7 days a week.

- ❑ Continue to collect new evidence and continually re-assessing the situation over time.

## SECTION SEVEN: ADDITIONAL INSTITUTION COMPONENTS

❑ Establish clear policies that enable the TAM Team to act on behalf of the institution.

❑ Establish policies that punish the following:

  ○ any acts of retaliation against someone reporting information to the TAM Team

  ○ the intentional provision of false information to the team or retaliation against those who have brought forward reasonable concerns

❑ Ensure that the above policies been made known to the entire campus community and are available on an ongoing basis.

❑ Ensure that your team has clear support from key administrators on campus.

❑ Ensure that all team members, including new members as they come in, received basic threat assessment training.

  ○ In-person training

  ○ Online/video training

  ○ Attending conference presentations by recognized experts

  ○ Attending workshops by recognized experts

  ○ Receiving training from regional subject matter experts

❑ Ensure that all team members have received advanced threat assessment training, after basic training has been completed.

  ○ Tabletop exercises

  ○ Refining current procedures and processes

❑ Make sure that the campus community can report threats to the team 24 hours a day, 7 days a week

❑ Provide the community with multiple means of reporting information to the team.

  ○ Phone line

  ○ Website

  ○ Periodic discussions with departments

❑ Take advantage of existing forms of communication as reporting mechanisms.

❑ Assess the college or university's emotional climate.

❑ Ensure that the institution promotes a proactive and safety-conscious campus.

❑ Provide general awareness training to the entire campus community on a periodic basis.

❑ Periodically confer with legal counsel about issues that may impact the team's work.

   ○ Laws and regulations

   ○ New developments from case law

   ○ Changes in regulations

❑ Identify and harness key liaison relationships with off-campus agencies, organizations, and businesses.

   ○ Local law enforcement

   ○ Social services

   ○ Community sports teams

   ○ Volunteer programs

   ○ Popular local gathering spots

❑ Identify and harness case management resources.

   ○ Counseling at the institution's mental health center

   ○ Evaluation and treatment through a local mental health professional

   ○ Involvement of law enforcement to contain or control the person in question.

   ○ Reduced course load

   ○ Medical leave of absence

   ○ Behavioral contracts

   ○ Involvement in community service

   ○ Assignment of a mentor

# APPENDIX C

## QUICK REFERENCE GUIDES

# APPENDIX C: QUICK REFERENCE GUIDES

## PRINCIPLES OF THREAT ASSESSMENT AND MANAGEMENT

The following principles guide threat assessment and management:[86]

### Principle 1: Targeted Violence Can Often Be Prevented
Perpetrators typically come up with an idea to do harm, develop a plan, acquire the means to do harm (e.g. get access to weapons), and then carry out the attack.[87] A TAM Team looks for information that may indicate that a person is on such a trajectory toward violence, and if so, the Team then determines where it might be able to intervene to prevent harm.

### Principle 2: Violence is a Dynamic Process
A TAM Team tries to determine the circumstances in which the person in question might pose a threat to himself or to others. A key aspect of the threat assessment and management process is to look ahead over the coming days, weeks, and months and see what in the person's life or situation might change — and how that change(s) might affect the likelihood of violence.

### Principle 3: Targeted Violence is a Function of Several Factors
Threat assessment should examine facts about the individual, the context of behavior, the environment in which the individual lives, the individual's current situation, factors that may precipitate violence or other negative behavior, and ways to make a target less accessible or vulnerable.

### Principle 4: Corroboration is Critical
Being skeptical about information received and corroborating information through multiple sources are critical to successful threat assessment and management.[88] This means that it is important to check facts where possible.

---

86  These principles come from Fein et al. (2002); Calhoun, F. & Weston, S. (June 2006); and from the experience of the primary authors.
87  Vossekuil et al., 2002.
88  Fein et al., 2002.

## Principle 5: Threat Assessment is about Behavior, not Profiles

There is no single "type" of person who perpetrates targeted violence.[89] Instead, threat assessment is evidence-based, focusing on the specific behaviors a person has exhibited and determining whether the person poses a threat (or is at risk) based upon those behaviors.[90]

## Principle 6: Cooperating Systems are Critical Resources

Communication, collaboration, and coordination among various departments and agencies are critical throughout the process of threat assessment and management. Using different systems throughout campus as well as outside resources provides more eyes and ears on the process of both assessing and managing a potentially violent situation.

## Principle 7: Does the Person Pose a Threat?

The central question of a threat assessment is whether the person in question *poses* a threat, NOT whether they *made* a threat.[91] A TAM Team should take *all* potential threatening behaviors seriously, not just those that have been verbalized or expressed in some other way. Similarly, just because a person has expressed intent to do harm does not necessarily mean that he/she poses a legitimate threat.

## Principle 8: Keep Victims in Mind

The TAM Team will need to pay attention to both victim safety and victim well-being. Victims are inherently more interested in threat management than threat assessment — meaning that they are more interested in what the Team will do to intervene, rather than what the particular assessment is. The TAM Team may need to devote time and energy to managing victim or witness fears.

## Principle 9: Early Identification and Intervention Helps Everyone

The earlier a concern is reported to the Team, the easier it is to address and resolve. Early identification also allows for a broader range of intervention options, especially those that are less punitive or control oriented.

---

89  Vossekuil et al., 2002.
90  Randazzo et al., 2006; Reddy et al., 2001.
91  Fein et al., 2002; Fein & Vossekuil, 1998; Fein, Vossekuil, & Holden (September 1995).

## Principle 10:
## Multiple Reporting Mechanisms Enhance Early Identification
The TAM Team should make it as easy as possible for the campus community to report concerns and for the Team to quickly access the resources it needs in order to intervene appropriately.

## Principle 11:
## Multi-Faceted Resources Can Provide Effective Interventions
Multiple strategies to de-escalate or contain the individual, connect the individual with the resources and assistance needed, reduce his/her access to the target, decrease the vulnerability of a potential target, and address situational or environmental factors should be used in concert in order to manage a threat.

## Principle 12:  Safety Is a Primary Focus
Safety is the primary goal of all threat assessment and management efforts. The TAM Team's ultimate purpose is to ensure the safety of the campus community by identifying and managing threats. Any particular interventions — counseling, support, confrontation, termination, arrest, hospitalization, etc. — are tools to achieve the goals of safety. They are not ends unto themselves.

### INQUIRY AND ASSESSMENT QUESTIONS

### Answer Key Inquiry Questions.[92]
Once the Team has gathered and documented the information it has collected, we recommend that the Team first use this information to answer several key inquiry questions.[93] These questions are designed to help organize the information gathered.

### What are the person's motive(s) and goals?
The purpose of this question is to understand the overall context of the behavior that first brought the person to the attention of the TAM Team, and also to understand whether those conditions or situation still exist. If those conditions still exist, the Team can use that information in crafting a management or referral/monitoring plan if necessary.

---

92  Fein et al., 2002.
93  These questions are taken largely from Fein et al. (2002) and have been modified for a higher education setting and to be used for faculty and staff who raise some concern, as well as for students. The guidance for how to weigh or interpret responses to the questions has been provided by the authors.

*Have there been any communications suggesting ideas or
intent to attack?*
If the Team finds that the person in question has communicated an idea
or plan to do harm — and that the source of that information is credible
— this is a strong indication that the person may be on a pathway toward
violence and therefore poses a threat. The Team should try to confirm or
corroborate this information through another source, or through other
information.

*Has the person shown inappropriate interest in any of the following?*
Workplace, school or campus attacks or attackers;
Weapons (including recent acquisition of any relevant weapon);
Incidents of mass violence (terrorism, workplace violence, mass
murderers);
Obsessive pursuit, stalking or monitoring others.
A "yes" to this question alone does not necessarily indicate that the
person in question poses a threat or is otherwise in need of some
assistance. Many people are interested in these topics but never pose any
threat. However, if a person shows some fascination or fixation on any of
these topics and has raised concern in another way, such as by expressing
an idea to do harm to others or to himself/herself, recently purchasing
a weapon, or showing helplessness or despair, the combination of these
facts should increase the Team's concern about the person in question.

*Has the person engaged in attack-related behaviors (i.e., any behavior
that moves an idea of harm forward toward actual harm)?*
If the Team determines that the person has engaged in any attack-related
behavior, this is an indication that the person is on a pathway toward
violence and has taken a step(s) forward toward carrying out an idea
to do harm. Any of these behaviors should prompt the Team to try to
corroborate or confirm these behaviors through other sources (or confirm
the reliability of the source reporting these behaviors). Any attack-related
behaviors should be seen as a serious indication of potential violence.

*Does the person have the capacity to carry out an act of
targeted violence?*
It is important for the Team to recognize that in some areas of the
country, it is quite common to own weapons and to have experience
using weapons from a young age. Therefore, what the Team should focus
on is the combination of the person owning or having access to

weapons AND some indication that the person has an idea or plan to do harm. Similarly, the Team should be concerned if the person develops an idea to do harm and THEN starts showing an interest in weapons. Either combination should raise the Team's concern, and move the Team toward determining that the person poses a threat.

### *Is the person experiencing hopelessness, desperation and/or despair?*

If the Team determines that the person in question is experiencing — or has recently experienced — desperation, hopelessness, and/or thoughts of suicide and there is NO other information indicating the person has thoughts or plans to harm other people, the Team should develop a plan to refer the person to necessary mental health care or emergency psychiatric intervention, possibly involving the institution's counseling center and/or police or local law enforcement if necessary. If the Team determines that the person in question is experiencing — or has recently experienced — desperation, hopelessness, and/or thoughts of suicide and there IS information that the person also has thoughts or plans to harm other people, the Team should determine that the person poses a threat and move to develop and implement a management plan to intervene with the person. The management plan should include resources to evaluate and treat the person's desperation and/or suicidal thoughts/plans.

### *Does the person have a trusting relationship with at least one responsible person (e.g., a friend, significant other, roommate, colleague, faculty advisor, coach, parent, etc.)?*

If the Team decides that the person in question poses a threat of harm, the Team can solicit the help of this responsible person. The responsible person can also be encouraged to take a more active role in discouraging the person from engaging in any harm — whether to himself/herself, others, or both.

### *Does the person see violence as an acceptable, desirable, or only way to solve problems?*

A "yes" to this question should increase the Team's concern about the person in question. But it should also lead the Team to consider what options they may have for helping the person solve their problems or improve their situation so that the person no longer looks toward violence to solve the problem.

### Is the person's conversation and "story" consistent with his or her actions?

If the TAM Team decides to interview the person of concern, the interview can be used as an opportunity to determine how forthcoming or truthful the person is being with the Team. The less forthcoming the person is, the more work the Team may have to do to develop an alliance if a management plan is needed.

### Are other people concerned about the person's potential for violence?

As people are often reluctant to see violence as a possibility, if the Team learns that someone in the person's life does think the person is capable of violence, this should raise the Team's concern considerably. However, the Team should recognize that those in close relationships with the person may be too close to the person/situation to admit violence is possible or even likely.

### What circumstances might affect the likelihood of violence?

All of us are capable of violence under the right (or wrong) circumstances. By asking this question, the Team can identify what factors in the person's life might change in the near- to mid-term, and whether those changes could make things better or worse for the person in question. If things look like they might improve for the person, the Team could monitor the person and situation for a while and re-assess after some time has passed. If things look like they might deteriorate, the Team can develop a management plan (if they believe the person poses a threat of harm or self-harm) or a referral plan (if the person does not pose a threat but appears in need of help) to help counteract the downturn in the person's circumstances.

### Where does the subject exist along the pathway to violence?

(See Figure 1 in Section Two)
Have they developed an idea to do harm?
Have they developed a plan?
Have they taken any steps toward implementing the plan?
Have they developed the capacity or means to carry out the plan?
How fast are they moving toward engaging in harm?
Where can the Team intervene to move the person off that pathway toward harm?

**Make the Assessment**.

Once the Team has answered the above questions (recognizing that a team may not be able to obtain information regarding all of the questions) and documented its answers, it then assesses the threat posed by the individual by answering the following two ultimate assessment questions:

**A. *Does the person pose a threat of harm, whether to him/herself, to others, or both? That is, does the person's behavior suggest that he or she is on a pathway toward harm?*** [94]

If the answer is "no," the Team documents its response and reasoning and proceeds to Question B. If the answer is "yes," the Team documents its response and rationale, and then proceeds to develop, implement, and continually monitor an individualized threat management plan to reduce the risk that the person poses. The Team should document the details of this plan, as well as document steps it takes to implement the plan and/or refer the person for help. The Team does not need to answer Question B.

**B. *If the person does not pose a threat of harm, does the person otherwise show a need for help or intervention, such as mental health care?***

If the answer is "no," the Team documents its response, records the person and incident in the Team's incident database, and closes the inquiry. If the answer is "yes," the Team documents its response and rationale, and then develops, implements, and re-evaluates a plan to monitor the person and situation and/or connect the person with resources in order to assist him/her with solving problems or addressing needs. The Team should document the details of this plan, as well as document steps taken to implement the plan and/or refer the person for help.

The answers to Questions A and B will dictate the Priority Level that the TAM Team assigns to the case. The Priority Level is designed to communicate both the level of threat posed by the person in question, as well as actions that may be necessary on the part of the Team to address and reduce that threat level. While the Team can choose its own rating scale, we offer the following for consideration.

---

94  Fein et al., 2002.

## Sample Priority Levels for Threat Cases

### Priority 1 (Extreme Risk)

The person/situation appears to pose a clear and immediate threat of serious violence toward self or others and requires containment. The Team should immediately notify law enforcement to pursue containment options, and/or take actions to protect identified target(s). Once such emergency actions have been taken, the Team shall then develop and implement a management plan in anticipation of the person's release or return to campus.

### Priority 2 (High Risk)

The person/situation appears to pose a threat of self-harm or physical violence, usually to an identifiable target, but currently lacks immediacy and/or a specific plan — or a specified plan of violence does exist but currently lacks a specific target. This requires the Team to develop and implement a management plan.

### Priority 3 (Moderate Risk)

The person/situation does not appear to pose a threat of violence or self-harm at this time, but does exhibit behaviors/circumstances that are likely to be disruptive to the community. This case warrants some intervention, referral and monitoring to minimize risk for significant disruption to the community or escalation in threat. The Team should develop a referral and/or active monitoring plan.

### Priority 4 (Low Risk)

The person/situation does not appear to pose a threat of violence or self-harm at this time, nor is their evidence of significant disruption to the community. This case may warrant some intervention, referral and monitoring to minimize risk for escalation in threat. The Team should develop a monitoring plan.

### Priority 5 (No Identified Risk)

The person/situation does not appear to pose a threat of violence or self-harm at this time, nor is their evidence of significant disruption to the community. The Team can close the case without a management or monitoring plan, following appropriate documentation.

# APPENDIX D

## SAMPLE POLICIES, PROCEDURES AND FORMS

# APPENDIX D:
# SAMPLE POLICIES, PROCEDURES AND FORMS

### SAMPLE ANTI-VIOLENCE POLICY FROM IOWA STATE UNIVERSITY

### Violence-Free Campus Policy

Effective Date: 12/4/2007
Contact: Iowa State University Police Division, Human Resource Services

### Introduction

The safety and security of the Iowa State University campus and community are very important. Our students, employees, and visitors should be able to pursue their education, work, and other activities in a safe, non-threatening environment. Unfortunately, violence can occur. To educate and empower all members of the University community, resources and procedures are in place to prevent, deter, and respond to concerns regarding acts of violence. Iowa State University also offers workshops to assist departments and individuals in detecting indicators for concern and resources to protect themselves and their environments. Safety is everyone's responsibility.

### Policy Statement

### Violence not Tolerated
Violence, threats or implied threats of violence, and intimidation (verbal or physical acts intended to frighten or coerce) impede the goal of providing a safe environment and will not be tolerated. All students, employees, and visitors are covered by this policy as well as the policies referenced below. This policy applies to conduct on "campus," which by definition is not limited to central campus but includes all property owned or used by the University.

### Weapons
As indicated in the policies below, weapons are not permitted on the campus except for purposes of law enforcement and as specially authorized for purposes of instruction, research, or service.

## Enforcement
The University will pursue disciplinary, student judicial, civil or criminal action as appropriate under the circumstances against any person who violates this policy by engaging in such violence, threats of violence, or intimidation.

## Reporting
Students, employees, and visitors should address emergencies by calling 911, whether they are on central campus or on other University property.

For all other non-emergency concerns of violence, the students, employees, and visitors should notify the Iowa State University Police Division at 294-4428. The Iowa State University Police Division is the central location for tracking concerns of violence – it is important that the Police Division is made aware of concerns of violence even if they occur on property outside of central campus.

The University has adopted procedures for responding to and addressing conduct that violates this policy and urges all students, employees and visitors to be alert to the possibility of violence on campus. As part of the University community, all students, employees, and visitors are responsible for reporting violence they experience or witness.

## Threat Management
The Critical Incident Response Team (CIRT) is an administrative group formed to promote awareness and responsiveness across campus to avoid or address situations that may involve violence, threats, intimidation, or property damage. In addition, a Threat Management Team, which is part of CIRT, may assist the Iowa State University Police Division and departments to assess situations involving the potential for violence. The Threat Management Team is staffed through the Iowa State University Police Division.

## Resources and Preparedness
Iowa State University, as part of its annual communication on safety, will inform individuals of this policy and its related procedures and resources.

## Confidentiality

Confidentiality of complaints and parties will be preserved to the greatest extent possible, understanding that the University may have an obligation to take some action even if the complainant is reluctant to proceed. Parties and witnesses to a complaint are also expected to maintain confidentiality of the matter, understanding that they will often not have all the facts and that they could impair the investigation by divulging information to persons outside of the investigatory process.

## Non-Retaliation and False Claims

The University prohibits retaliation against persons who in good faith report violations of this policy or cooperate in an investigation. The University also prohibits the filing of knowingly false or misleading reports and providing knowingly false or misleading information in an investigation. Discipline or other action can result from either of these acts in violation of this policy.

## Resources

> Procedures
> Iowa State University Police Division
> Human Resource Services
> Dean of Students
> Employee Assistance Program
> Student Counseling Center

## Other Links Addressing Violence

Iowa Administrative Code
Section 681-9—Uniform Rules of Personal Conduct
Section 681-13.14—General Rules on Use of Grounds and Facilities
Section 681—13.16(262)—Conduct at public events
> Iowa Criminal Code (beginning with Chapter 701)
Faculty Handbook:
7.2.2.4. Criminal Acts or Violence
Student Conduct Code:
4.2.3 Assault, Injury and Threat
4.2.14 Sexual Assault or Abuse
4.2.17 Possession or Misuse of Weapons
4.2.7 Public Disorder, Group Violence and Mass Disruptions

## Policies Regarding Weapons

Iowa Administrative Code
Section 681-13.14(5)
Student Conduct Code:
4.2.17 Possession or Misuse of Weapons
        Policy Library: Facilities and Ground Use, Activities

## Non-Retaliation

Policy Library: Non-retaliation

## Sample Anti-Violence Procedures from Iowa State University

Procedures for Supporting a Violence-Free Campus

As part of Iowa State University's policy on a Violence-Free Campus, the University has adopted the following procedures and resources that students, employees, and visitors may use to prevent and address acts of violence, threats, and intimidation.

### Stop Immediate Threat or Harm – Report It

**You should call 911 for emergencies.**  Please do not ignore or disregard violence or threats against you or others – the University needs your assistance to make our campus safe.

If you are experiencing or observing an immediate threatening or violent situation, you are responsible for alerting local enforcement as soon as you are able.  Delaying your report may unnecessarily allow the behavior to continue, harm your own well-being, or jeopardize the investigation due to the passage of time, fading memories, or departure of witnesses.

The central location for tracking reported concerns of violence is the Iowa State University Police Division.  In all cases, it is important that the Iowa State University Police Division is informed of the concern either through you or local law enforcement personnel.  You can reach the Iowa State University Police Division by calling 294-4428.

### Other Complaints

As a member of the University community, you are also encouraged to report other behavior that is unusual or threatening even if you do not perceive the risk as immediately dangerous or imminent.  To report other concerns that may not pose immediate threats, call the Iowa State University Police Division (294-4428).

If you have concerns over the conduct of a student, employee or visitor on campus, you may also inform the following persons in addition to notifying the Iowa State University Police Division:
your supervisor, if the concern is about a student, employee or visitor
the Director of Human Resource Services, if the concern is about an employee
the Dean of Students  Office , if the concern is about a student

In all cases, be sure to communicate that you feel the behavior involves violence or a violation of the policy on a Violence-Free Campus. You may be asked to provide your complaint in writing.

If a supervisor receives a complaint that the policy on a Violence-Free Campus has been violated, the supervisor is responsible for informing the Iowa State University Police Division. The supervisor should also coordinate with the Department of Human Resource Services or the Dean of Students as appropriate to make sure the complaint is addressed. If disciplinary action against the accused is required, such action shall be taken in accordance with the applicable contract, policy, or handbook for that person's classification.

## Preparedness: How You Can Help Prevent and Mitigate Violent Situations

Do not ignore a potentially violent situation. On the other hand, do not unnecessarily put yourself at risk of danger – call the Iowa State University Police Division at 294-4428 or local law enforcement at 911.

The Iowa State University Police Division can offer you, your group, or your department education on how to avoid finding yourself in a violent situation and what to do should a violent situation arise. Some of the programs offered cover sexual assault, workplace safety, and travel safety. More information regarding educational training programs can be found at *http://www.dps.iastate.edu/wordpress/?page_id=114*.

## Management of Concerns

The Critical Incident Response Team (CIRT) is an administrative group formed to promote awareness and responsiveness across campus to avoid or address situations that may involve violence, threats, or intimidation. In addition, a Threat Management Team, which is part of CIRT, may assist the Iowa State University Police Division and departments to assess the potential for violence and to recommend interventions to de-escalate and prevent such situations where that is possible. CIRT is a confidential body, so while CIRT may be working to address a situation, it may not be able to publicly disclose its assessment, plans, or actions.

Similarly, while the University, including the Iowa State University Police Division, will work with the complainant to keep him or her informed of the investigation and procedures, please understand that not all action taken against an accused can be revealed if it is confidential. If you have questions about a complaint you have made, you may contact the Iowa State University Police Division to see if there is any information that can be released.

## Recovery from Violent Situation

After a violent situation occurs, the affected employees, students, or families may often face difficulties in resolving their feelings and concerns. As situations are assessed, CIRT can facilitate group discussions or debriefing sessions as needed for the affected area to provide some understanding of and closure to the situation. The affected students or employees could also seek assistance from CIRT in the recovery process. Please also know that the Employee Assistance Program and the Student Counseling Center are available as a resource.

## Protective Orders/Restraining Orders Issued by a Court

If you have a protective order or restraining order that covers you at work, you should notify your supervisor and provide a copy of the order to the Iowa State University Police Division.

## Interim Measure/Restrictions

In some cases, it may be reasonable for the University to take interim measures or impose restrictions on contact with persons who may be subject to a threat of violence. In addition, the University may also revoke permission of persons violating this policy from remaining on campus. [Link: Iowa Admin Code § 681-13.19]

## Additional Resources

Policy
Iowa State University Police Division
Human Resource Services
Dean of Students
Employee Assistance Program
Student Counseling Center
Iowa Administrative Code § 681-13.19

# SAMPLE INCIDENT REPORT FORM

**Sample Incident Report Form**

**Report Information**

| Date of Report: | Day of Week: | ○ Monday  ○ Tuesday  ○ Wednesday  ○ Thursday<br>○ Friday  ○ Saturday  ○ Sunday | Time: _____ | ○ AM<br>○ PM |
|---|---|---|---|---|
| Report Taken by: | | Position: | | |

**Incident Information**

| Date of Incident: | Day of Week: | ○ Monday  ○ Tuesday  ○ Wednesday  ○ Thursday<br>○ Friday  ○ Saturday  ○ Sunday | Time: _____ | ○ AM<br>○ PM |
|---|---|---|---|---|
| Incident Location: | | | | |

**Reporting Party Information:**

| Last Name: | | First Name: | MI: |
|---|---|---|---|
| AKA: | | Sex: ☐ Male ☐ Female | DOB: | Age: |
| Ethnicity: ☐ African American/Black  ☐ Caucasian American/White  ☐ Native American<br>☐ Asian American  ☐ Hispanic American/Latino  ☐ Other:_____ | | | |
| Home Address: | | Home Phone: | |
| City: | State: | ZIP Code: | Mobile Phone: |
| Employer: | Position: | Classification: ☐ Faculty ☐ Staff<br>☐ Student ☐ Other____ | |
| Work Address: | | Work Phone: | |

**Victim Information (if different than reporting party):**

| Last Name: | | First Name: | MI: |
|---|---|---|---|
| AKA: | | Sex: ☐ Male ☐ Female | DOB: | Age: |
| Ethnicity: ☐ African American/Black  ☐ Caucasian American/White  ☐ Native American<br>☐ Asian American  ☐ Hispanic American/Latino  ☐ Other:_____ | | | |
| Home Address: | | Home Phone: | |
| City: | State: | ZIP Code: | Mobile Phone: |
| Employer: | Position: | Classification: ☐ Faculty ☐ Staff<br>☐ Student ☐ Other____ | |
| Work Address: | | Work Phone: | |

**Subject Information**

| Last Name: | | First Name: | MI: |
|---|---|---|---|
| AKA: | | Sex: ☐ Male ☐ Female | DOB: | Age: |
| Ethnicity: ☐ African American/Black  ☐ Caucasian American/White  ☐ Native American<br>☐ Asian American  ☐ Hispanic American/Latino  ☐ Other:_____ | | | |
| Home Address: | | Home Phone: | |
| City: | State: | ZIP Code: | Mobile Phone: |
| Employer: | Position: | Classification: ☐ Faculty ☐ Staff<br>☐ Student ☐ Other____ | |
| Work Address: | | Work Phone: | |

**Witness Information:**

| Name | Position | Address | Phone |
|------|----------|---------|-------|
|  |  |  |  |
|  |  |  |  |
|  |  |  |  |

**Describe the incident in detail (what was said/done, who was involved, when, where, why, and how)**

Was victim injured?  ☐ No  ☐ Yes  ☐ Unknown          Did victim require medical attention?  ☐ No  ☐ Yes  ☐ Unknown

Was a weapon involved?  ☐ No  ☐ Yes  ☐ Unknown          Type of Weapon?  ☐ Firearm  ☐ Knife  ☐ Other:_____

**Does subject have any prior history of violence?**  ☐ No  ☐ Yes  ☐ Unknown

Describe known history of violence or weapons concerns:

**Does subject have any prior criminal or disciplinary problems?**  ☐ No  ☐ Yes  ☐ Unknown

Describe history:

**Is subject struggling with or facing any other known stressors ?**  ☐ No  ☐ Yes  ☐ Unknown

Describe:

# SAMPLE THREAT ASSESSMENT & MANAGEMENT TEAM CASE REVIEW SHEET

**Sample Threat Assessment & Management Team Case Review Sheet**

| Case #: | Subject Name: | Date of Review: |
|---|---|---|

| Priority Level | Comments | | |
|---|---|---|---|
| ○ Priority 1 (Imminent Risk) | | | |
| ○ Priority 2 (High Risk) | | | |
| ○ Priority 3 (Moderate Risk) | | | |
| ○ Priority 4 (Low Risk) | | | |
| ○ Priority 5 (No Identified Risk) | | | |
| ○ Insufficient Information | | | |

| Management Strategies | Comments | Assigned To: | Date Completed: |
|---|---|---|---|
| ○ Monitor – Passive | | | |
| ○ Monitor – Active | | | |
| ○ Subject Interview | | | |
| ○ Involve Subject Support Systems | | | |
| ○ Trusted ally | | | |
| ○ Parent / Family | | | |
| ○ Victim Interview | | | |
| ○ Suspension | | | |
| ○ Termination | | | |
| ○ Bar Subject from Premises | | | |
| ○ Bar Subject from Contacting Victim | | | |
| ○ Civil Order | | | |
| ○ Mental Health Commitment – | | | |
| ○ Voluntary | | | |
| ○ Involuntary | | | |
| ○ Fitness for Duty Evaluation | | | |
| ○ Refer for Criminal Investigation | | | |
| ○ Refer for Disciplinary Action | | | |
| ○ Notification for Safety Planning | | | |
| ○ Target | | | |
| ○ Target Spouse/Family | | | |
| ○ Campus/Workplace Officials | | | |
| ○ Law Enforcement Agencies | | | |
| ○ Refer to Student Assistance | | | |
| ○ Dean of Students | | | |
| ○ Disability Resources | | | |
| ○ Faculty / Academic Advisor | | | |
| ○ Residence Hall | | | |
| ○ Student Counseling | | | |
| ○ Student Health | | | |
| ○ Other _____ | | | |
| ○ Refer to Faculty/Staff Assistance | | | |
| ○ Provost/Academic Affairs | | | |
| ○ Human Resource Services | | | |
| ○ Equal Opportunity & Diversity | | | |
| ○ EAP | | | |
| ○ Other _____ | | | |

**General Comments**

Case Review Conducted By:

_____          Date: _____

Team Leader

# SAMPLE NOTICE OF NO CONTACT

**Sample Notice of No Contact**

[Date]

[Address]

Dear _____:

The _____ University Police Department has received a report from _____ that you have continued to correspond with him/her both by telephone and electronic mail (e-mail) even after he/she requested that you to stop such communication. _____ indicated that your repeated contacts have caused alarm and unreasonable distress.

This type of conduct, which it has been reported that you engaged in, cannot and will not be tolerated. In light of these allegations and the concerns expressed, effective <u>immediately</u>, you are being placed on formal notice that you are not allowed to communicate directly with _____ by telephone, electronic mail, telegraph, in writing, in person or through third persons. Any contact with _____ could result in harassment or criminal trespass charges being filed against you.

The following paragraphs list subsections of the [INSERT REFERENCE TO STATE LAW OR INSTITUTIONAL POLICY HERE] that apply to the allegations against you:

[INSERT CITATION OF LAW OR INSTITUTIONAL POLICY HERE]

**[E.g.] 708.7 Harassment.**
A person commits harassment when, with intent to intimidate, annoy, or alarm another person, the person does any of the following:

Communicates with another by telephone, telegraph, or writing without legitimate purpose and in a manner likely to cause the other person annoyance or harm.
A person commits harassment when the person, purposefully and without legitimate purpose, has personal contact with another person, with the intent to threaten, intimidate, or alarm that other person. As used in this section, unless the context otherwise requires, "personal contact" means an encounter in which two or more people are in visual or physical proximity to each other. "Personal contact" does not require a physical touching or oral communication, although it may include these types of contacts.
A person commits harassment in the first degree when the person commits harassment involving a threat to commit a forcible felony, or commits harassment and has previously been convicted of harassment three or more times under this section or any similar statute during the preceding ten years. Harassment in the first degree is an aggravated misdemeanor.
A person commits harassment in the second degree when the person commits harassment involving a threat to commit bodily injury, or commits harassment and has previously been convicted of harassment two times under this section or any similar statute during the preceding ten years. Harassment in the second degree is a serious misdemeanor.
Any other act of harassment is harassment in the third degree. Harassment in the third degree is a simple misdemeanor.

The criminal trespass statute provides, in part, as follows:

**716.7 Trespass defined.**
The term "property" shall include any land, dwelling, building, conveyance, vehicle or other temporary or permanent structure whether publicly or privately owned.

2

The term "trespass" shall mean one or more of the following acts:

Entering or remaining upon or in property without justification after being notified or requested to abstain from entering or to remove or vacate therefrom by the owner, lessee, or person in lawful possession, or the agent or employee of the owner, lessee, or person in lawful possession, or by any peace officer, magistrate, or public employee whose duty it is to supervise the use or maintenance of the property.
Entering upon or in property for the purpose or with the effect of unduly interfering with the lawful use of the property by others.

If you need to communicate with _____ for any reason, you must first make arrangements with _____. You must be prepared to substantiate your request. You may contact _____ by calling the _____ University Police Department at [phone number] during regular business hours.

Please understand that a violation of the statute referenced above could result in criminal prosecution against you. It could also result in university disciplinary action being brought against you by the Judicial Affairs Division of the Dean of Students Office. This information is being provided in an attempt to educate you to the consequences of such actions and to prevent any future problems.

Sincerely,


_____ University Police Department


cc:     [List member of TAM Team that have need to know]
        files

# SAMPLE THREAT ASSESSMENT AND MANAGEMENT TEAM FEEDBACK AND EVALUATION FORM

**Sample Threat Assessment and Management Team
Feedback and Evaluation Form**

This memo is a request for feedback about your recent contact with the Threat Assessment & Management Team. The Team is committed to enhancing the safety and well-being of the campus community. The Team operates to ensure that the institution responds in a coordinated, timely and effective manner in enhancing community safety.

As part of continuously evaluating and improving the services provided by the Team, we ask for your feedback regarding your experience.

**Your Classification:** ☐ Faculty ☐ Staff ☐ Student ☐ Other

**Prior to this situation, I was aware of the existence and purpose of the Threat Assessment & Management Team:** ☐ Yes ☐ No

|  | Strongly Disagree | Disagree | Neutral | Agree | Strongly Agree |
|---|---|---|---|---|---|
| Team members were committed to enhancing the safety of my situation. | ☐ | ☐ | ☐ | ☐ | ☐ |
| Team members responded in a timely manner to my initial concerns. | ☐ | ☐ | ☐ | ☐ | ☐ |
| The Team's purpose and operation were clear to me. | ☐ | ☐ | ☐ | ☐ | ☐ |
| Team efforts contributed to decreased concerns about the situation. | ☐ | ☐ | ☐ | ☐ | ☐ |
| Team members maintained a fair and objective approach to the situation. | ☐ | ☐ | ☐ | ☐ | ☐ |
| I am satisfied regarding my involvement with the Team. | ☐ | ☐ | ☐ | ☐ | ☐ |

What was the most valuable resource or response from the Team?

Aside from the immediate response from the Team, was there any other positive impact to the work climate that resulted?

Were you comfortable and able to describe your concerns for the group?

Do you have suggestions about how the Team can be more effective in responding to situations like these?

# APPENDIX E

## ADDITIONAL RESOURCES

# APPENDIX E: ADDITIONAL RESOURCES

**Additional Resources and Suggested Reading**

Association of Threat Assessment Professionals (2006). Risk assessment guideline elements for violence: Considerations for assessing the risk of future violent behavior. Los Angeles: Authors.

Braverman, M. (1999). Preventing workplace violence: A guide for employers and practitioners. London: Sage.

Calhoun, F.S. & Weston, S.W. (2003). Contemporary threat management: A practical guide for identifying, assessing and managing individuals of violent intent. San Diego: Specialized Training Services.

Corcoran, M.H. & Cawood, J.S. (2003). Violence assessment and intervention: The practitioner's handbook. New York: CRC.

DeBecker, G. (1997). The gift of fear: And other survival signals that protect us from violence. New York: Dell.

Fein, R., Vossekuil, B., Pollack, W., Borum, R., Modzeleski, W., & Reddy, M. (2002). Threat assessment in schools: A guide to managing threatening situations and to creating safe school climates. Washington, DC: U.S. Department of Education and U.S. Secret Service.

Flannery, R.B. (1995). Violence in the workplace. New York: Crossroad.

Hoffman, A.M., Schuh, J.H., & Fenske, R.H. (Eds.). (1998). Violence on campus: Defining the problems, strategies for action. Gaithersburg, MD: Aspen.

International Association of Campus Law Enforcement Administrators. (1993). Handling institutional violence on campus. Hartford, CT: IACLEA.

International Association of Campus Law Enforcement Administrators. (1996). Handling violence in the workplace. Hartford, CT: IACLEA.

Lazenby, R. (Ed.). (2007). April 16: Virginia Tech remembers. New York: Plume.

Meloy, J.R. (2000). Violence risk and threat assessment. San Diego, Specialized Training Services.

Mohandie, K. (2000). School violence threat management. San Diego: Specialized Training Services.

Monahan, J., Steadman, H.J., Silver, E., & Applebaum, P.S. (2001). Rethinking risk assessment: The MacArthur study of mental disorder and violence. New York: Oxford.

Monahan, J. (1995). The clinical prediction of violent behavior. London: J. Aronson.

O'Neill, D., Fox, J., Depue, R., Englander, E., et al. (2008). Campus violence prevention and response: Best practices for Massachusetts Higher Education. Boston, MA: Massachusetts Department of Higher Education.

Pavela, G. The Pavela Report. Available at http://collegepubs.com/the_pavela_report.

Quinsey, V.L., Harris, G.T., Rice, M.E. & Cormier, C.A. (1998). Violent offenders: Appraising and managing risk. Washington, DC: American Psychological Association.

The Jed Foundation (2008). Student mental health and the law: A resource for institutions of higher education. New York, NY: The Jed Foundation.

Vossekuil, B., Fein, R., Reddy, M., Borum, R., & Modzeleski, W. (2002). The final report and findings of the Safe School Initiative: Implications for the prevention of school attacks in the United States. Washington, DC: U.S. Department of Education and U.S. Secret Service.

**Reports Written on College and University Security**

- Report and recommendations of Task Force on School and Campus Safety, National Association of Attorneys General, 2007. *http://www.ago.state.ms.us/images/uploads/forms/NAAG-SchoolSafety.pdf*

- National Summit on Campus Public Safety: Strategies for Colleges and Universities in a Homeland Security Environment; COPS, 2005. *http://www.cops.usdoj.gov/files/ric/Publications/ NationalSummitonCampusPublicSafety.pdf*

- Expecting the Unexpected: Lessons from the Virginia Tech Tragedy; American Association of State Colleges and Universities, 2007. *http://www.aascu.org/media/pdf/07_expectingunexpected.pdf*

- Gubernatorial Task Force for University Campus Safety, Report on Findings and Recommendations, State of Florida, 2007. *http://www.dcf.state.fl.us/campussecurity/docs/finalReport052407. pdf*

- Overview of the Virginia Tech Tragedy and Implications for Campus Safety: The IACLEA Blueprint for Safer Campuses. The International Association of Campus Law Enforcement Administrators, 2008. *http://www.iaclea.org/Visitors/PDFs/VT-taskforce-report_Virginia-Tech.pdf*

- State of Illinois Campus Security Task Force Report to the Governor, 2008. *http://www.ready.illinois.gov/pdf/CSTF_Report_ExecutiveSummary. pdf*

- Report to the Governor: Examination of Safety and Security at Kentucky's Public and Private Postsecondary Institutions; Governor's Task Force on Campus Safety, 2007. *http://www.ppc.ky.gov/NR/rdonlyres/34C366A3-6A6C-4131-A5DA-42F462A48377/0/GovernorTaskForceReport.pdf*

- Securing our Future: Making Colleges and Universities Safe Places to Learn and Grow; Missouri Campus Security Task Force, 2007. *http://www.dps.mo.gov/CampusSafety/GovernorsFinalReport.pdf*

- New Jersey Campus Security Task Force Report Submitted to Governor Jon S. Corzine, 2007. *http://www.njohsp.gov/press/10-02-07-campus-security.pdf*

- Recommendations for Action: Emergency Preparedness in Higher Education; New Mexico Governor's Task Force on Campus Safety, 2007 *http://oja.wi.gov/docview.asp?docid=11845&locid=97*

- Final Report, Subcommittee on Mitigation, Protocols, and Infrastructure, New Mexico Governor's Task Force on Campus Safety, 2008. *http://hed.state.nm.us/cms/kunde/rts/hedstatenmus/ docs/1060117949-04-14-2008-11-01-12.htm*

- Campus Safety and Security Task Force Final Report, Norfolk State University, 2007.
  *http://www.nsu.edu/itsyourbusiness/pdf/ CampusSafetyandSecurityFinalReport.pdf*

- Report to the Campus Safety Task Force Presented to Attorney General Roy Cooper, North Carolina, 2008.
  *http://www.ncdoj.gov/DocumentStreamerClient?directory=Whats New/&file=CampusSafetyReport_LR.pdf*

- Campus Life and Safety and Security Task Force (CLASS) Final Report, Oklahoma, 2008.
  *http://www.okhighered.org/class/final-report.pdf*

- Pennsylvania College Campus Security Assessment Report; Pennsylvania State Police, 2007.
  *http://www.psp.state.pa.us/psp/lib/psp/CampusAssessmentRpt.pdf*

- Report to the President: On Issues Raised by the Virginia Tech Tragedy; Leavitt, Gonzales, & Spellings, 2007.
  *http://www.hhs.gov/vtreport.pdf*

- The Report of the University of California Campus Security Task Force; University of California Office of the President, 2008.
  *http://www.ucop.edu/riskmgt/emergprep/documents/cstf_rpt.pdf*

- The University of North Carolina Campus Safety Task Force Report to the President, 2007.
  *https://www.northcarolina.edu/content.php/safety_taskforce/index. htm*

- Mass shootings at Virginia Tech, Report of the Review Panel presented to Governor Kaine, Commonwealth of Virginia, 2007.
  *http://www.vtreviewpanel.org/report/index.html*

- Findings and Recommendations of the Virginia Working Group for Virginia Tech President Charles Steger, 2007.
  *http://www.vtnews.vt.edu/documents/2007-08-22_niles.doc*

- Governor's Task Force on Campus Safety, Final Report, Wisconsin, 2007
  *ftp://doaftp04.doa.state.wi.us/doadocs/ governorstaskforcecampussafetyfinalreport.pdf*